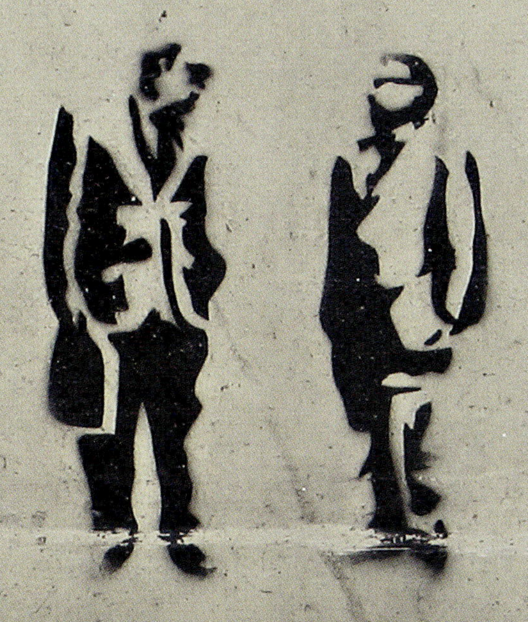

AF530781

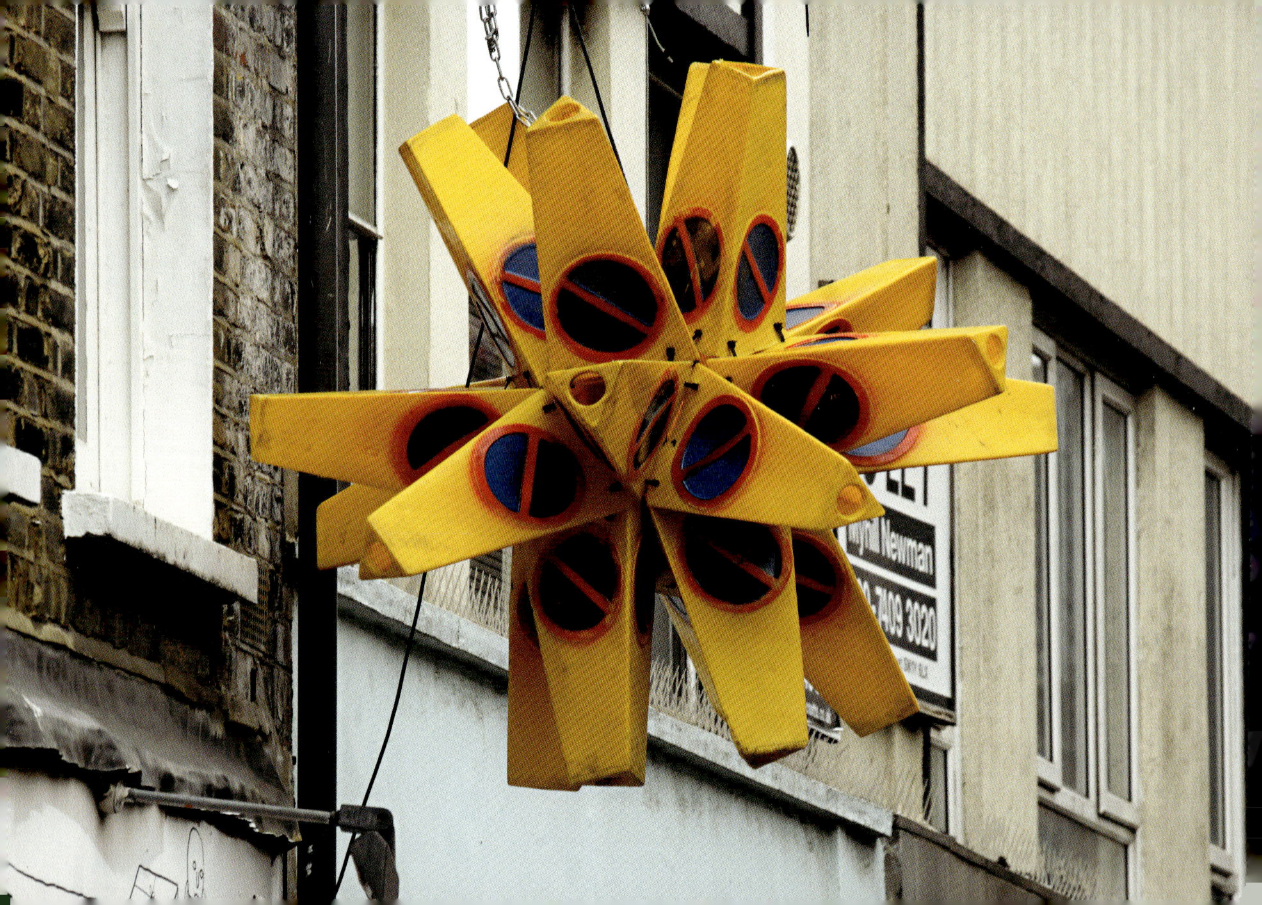
Newman
7409 3020

Alex MacNaughton

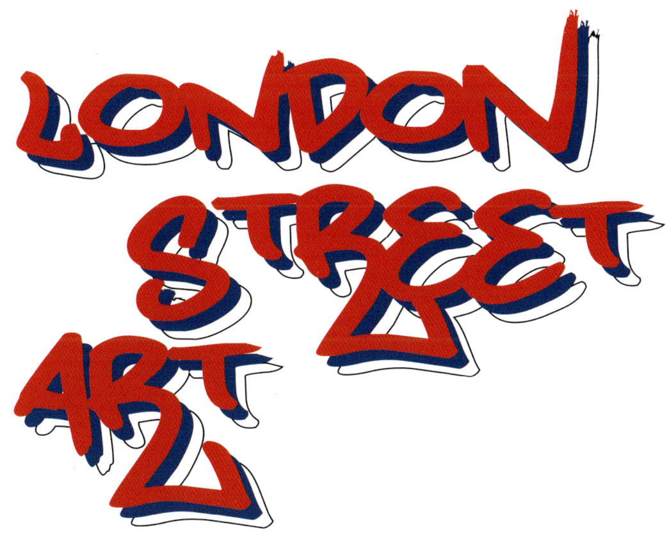

PRESTEL
Munich · Berlin · London · New York

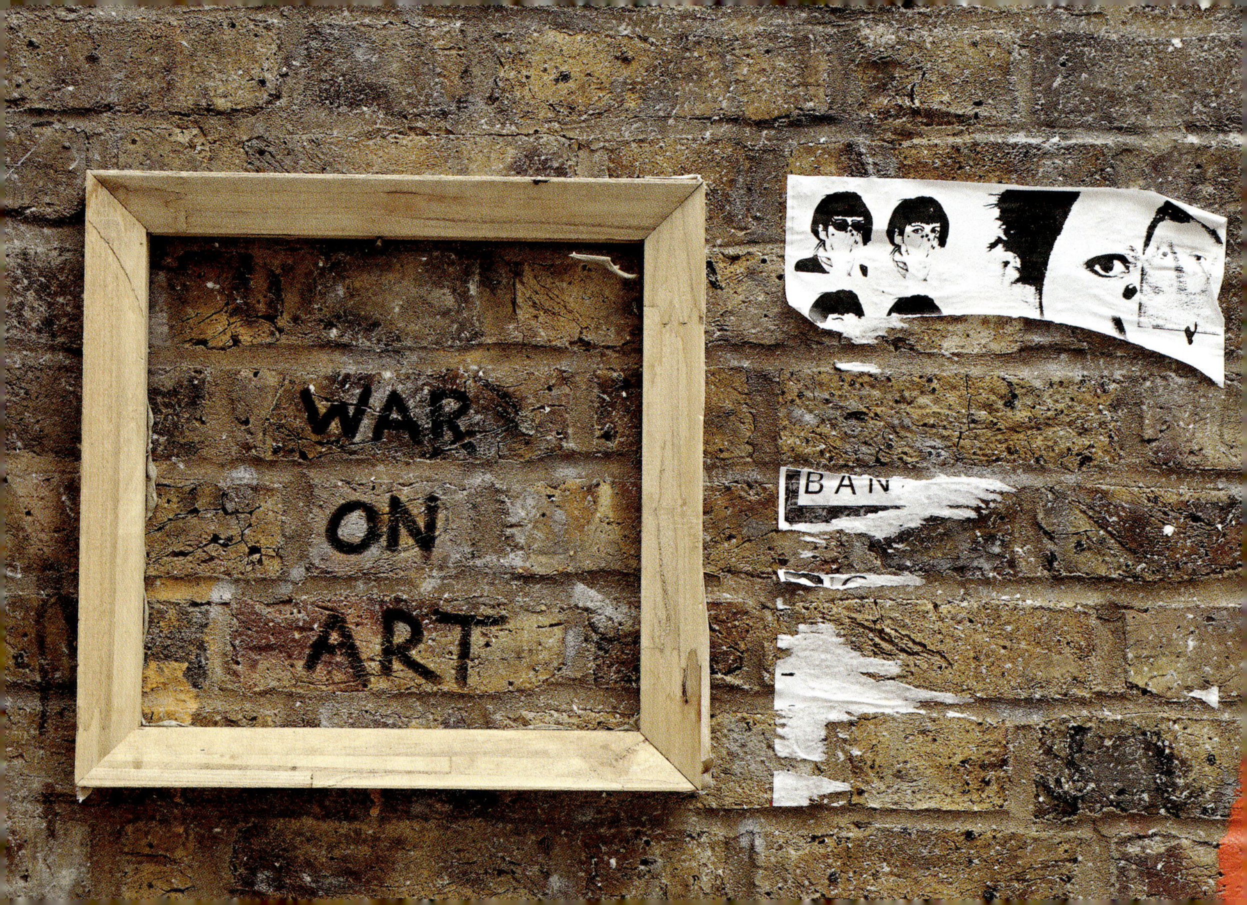
WAR
ON
ART
BAN

Introduction

Where does street art begin and graffiti finish? This is one of the great questions of our time, on a par with: How the hell did George Bush become president?

Many people will say that there is no such thing as street art and that it is just vandalism by another name. But a well-placed piece of street art can make you smile, laugh or think about what it is to be human in our modern world. Take a look at 'i-need', the starving African child with his iPod.

The art shown in this book breaks down into two main types: reproducible and freehand. The reproducible is the easier of the two to distinguish from graffiti as it consists of stencils and poster art that can be reproduced infinitely. Indeed, much of the work in creating reproducible street art takes place away from the street, which is used as both canvas and gallery for the work.

The freehand art, on the other hand, is much closer to graffiti, as all the work takes place on the street. I decided what freehand work to include mainly based on its complexity and whether the artist was following a theme, for example the 'big letter' series. Some artists work in both genres, such as *londonfrontline*, whose ‘evil monkey’ series started off as a number of freehand pieces before developing into a poster series.

When you compare the two genres, the greater use of colour in the freehand form is very obvious. This is mainly because of the difficulty of spraying stencils with a large number of colours. They rarely use more than two.

Equally the way the artist decides to place their work has a major effect on how it is interpreted. Some art appears to be placed with no reference to its surroundings, where other works seem deliberately placed to subvert them. The placement seems to add to its meaning, although this may be in the viewer’s imagination.

As street art ages it slowly gathers a patina from its environment, either by people adding to the original work (see the ‘Banksy can fuck off’ speech bubble), or simply by environmental wear and tear. The final stage of life for a piece of street art is often its removal, leaving a ghostly impression that can last a great deal longer than the original work.

Alex MacNaughton, July 2006

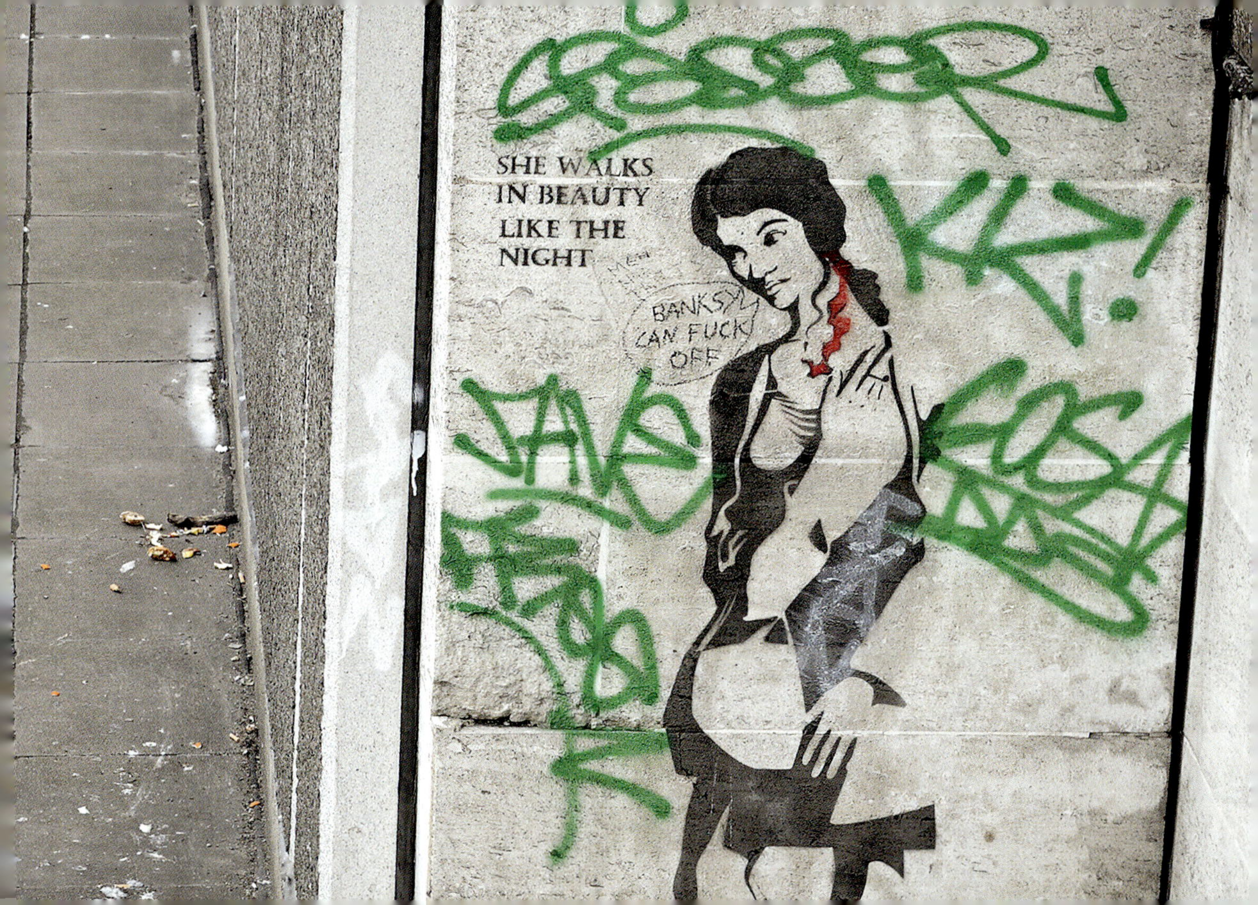
SHE WALKS
IN BEAUTY
LIKE THE
NIGHT
BANKSY
CAN FUCK
OFF

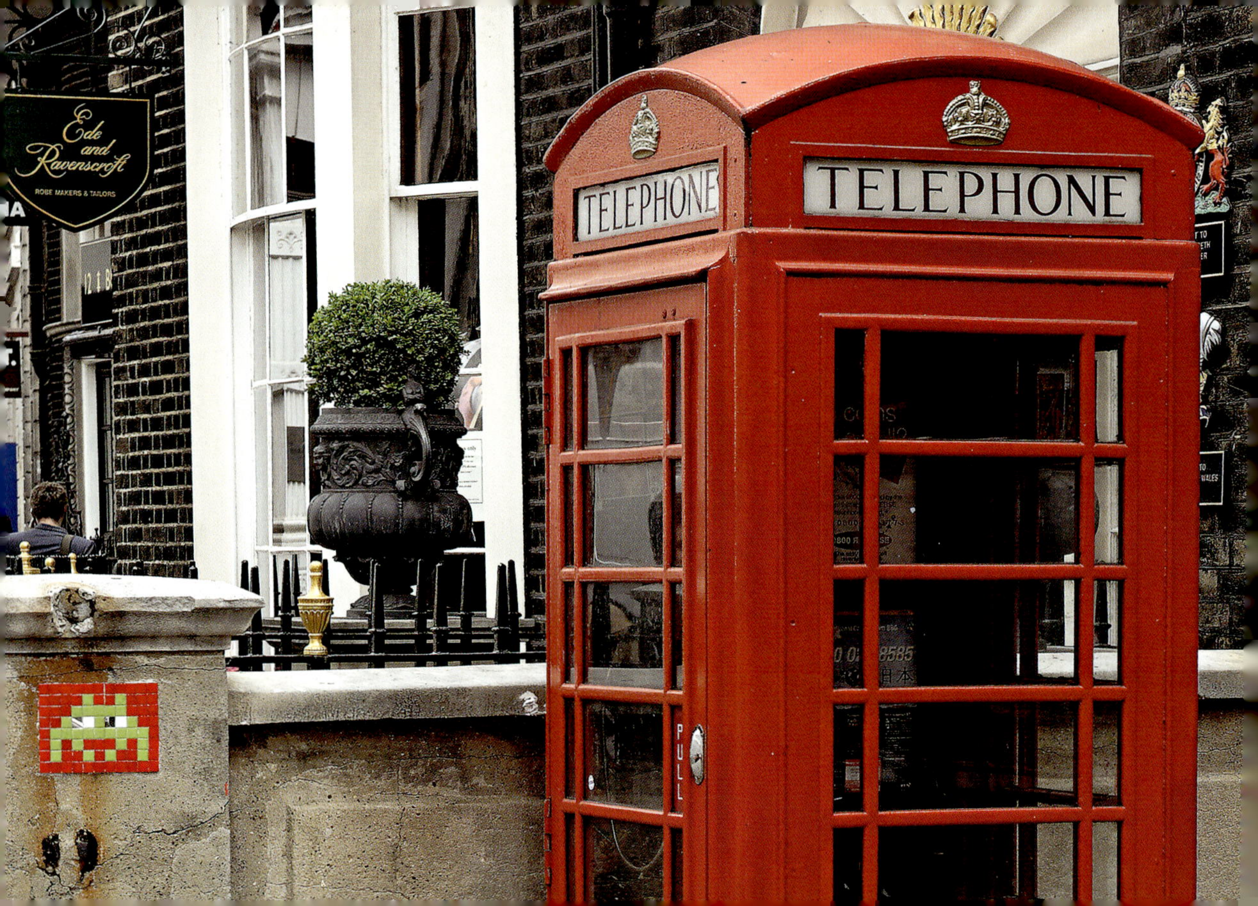
Ede and Ravenscroft
ROBE MAKERS & TAILORS
TELEPHONE
TELEPHONE
PULL

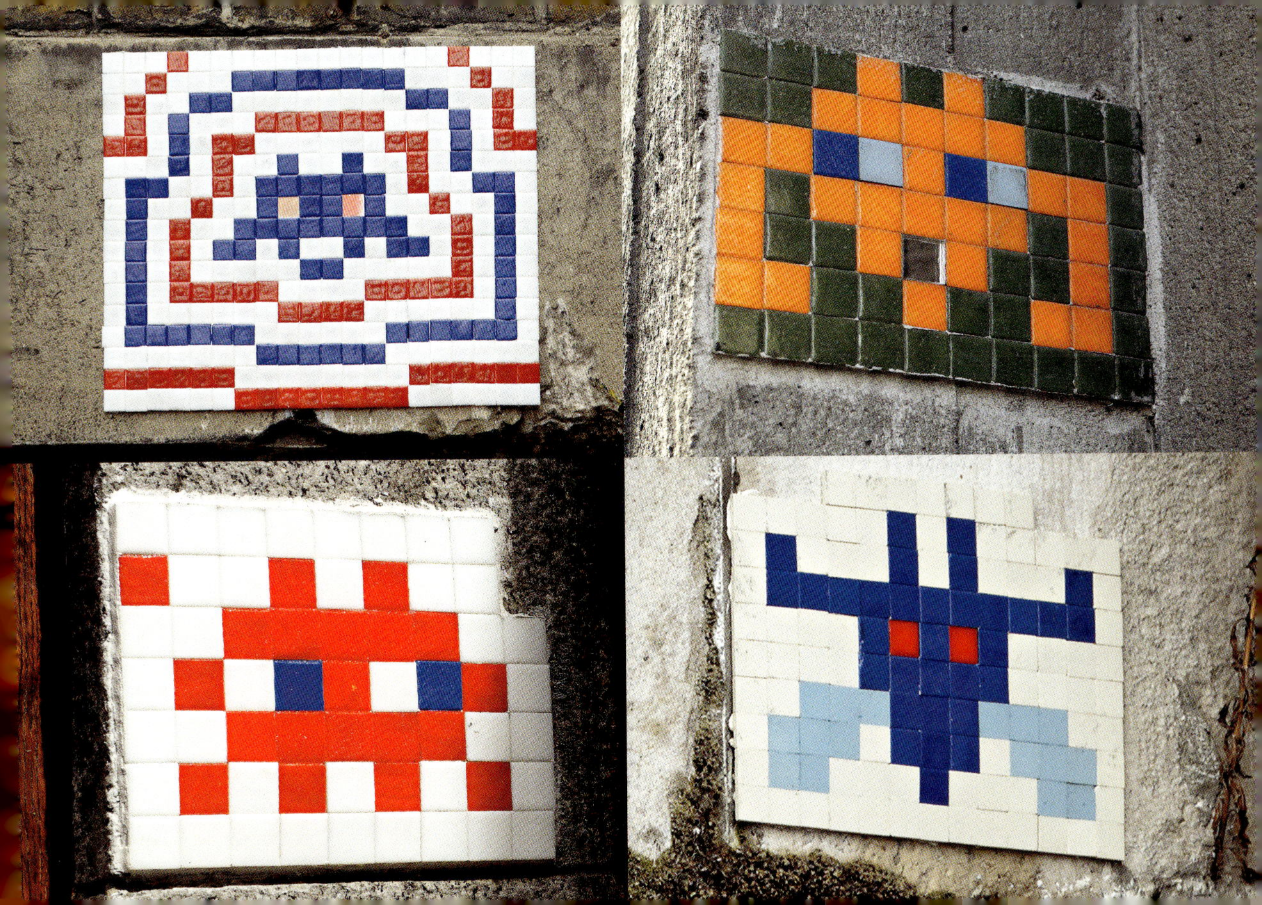

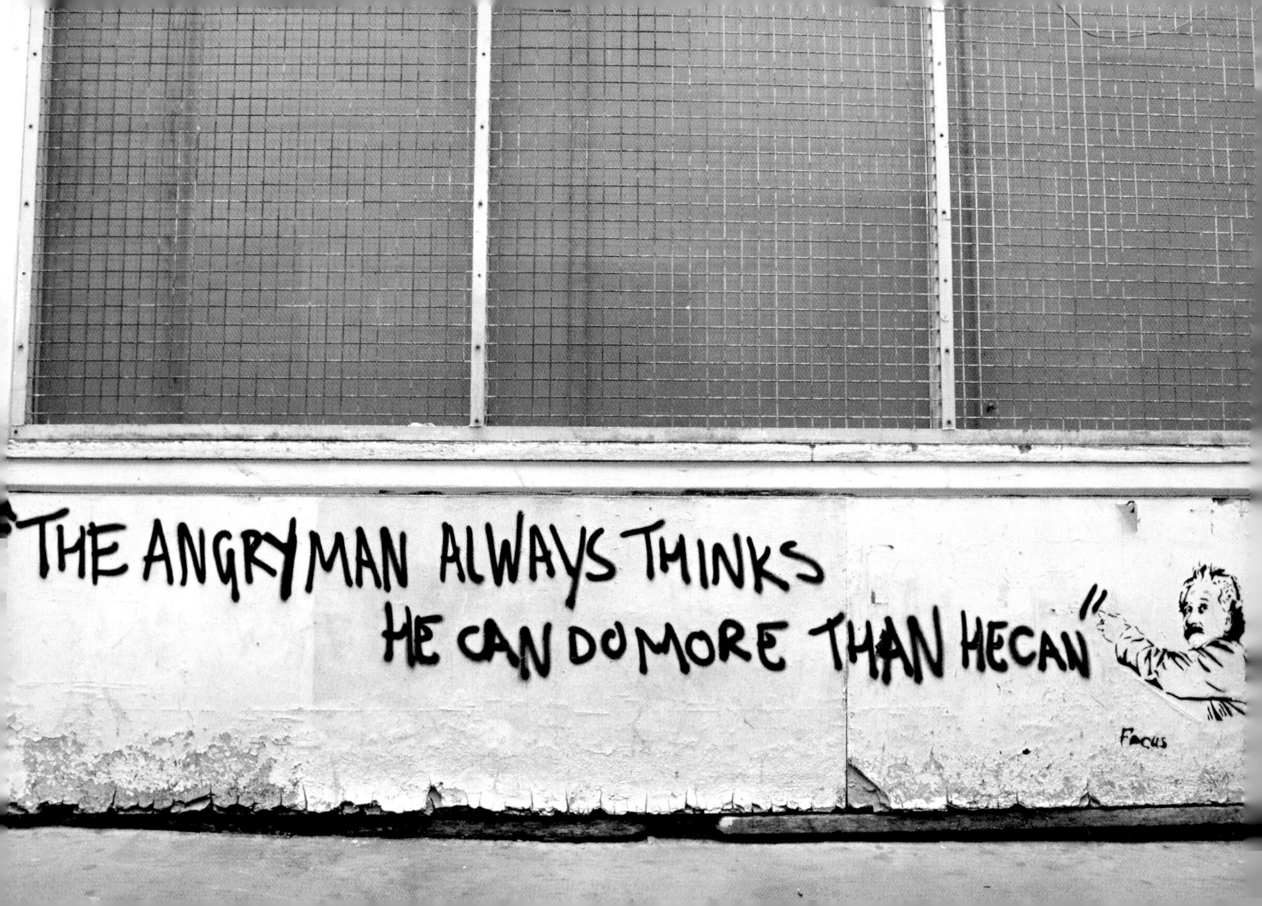

"THE ANGRY MAN ALWAYS THINKS
HE CAN DO MORE THAN HE CAN"

Focus

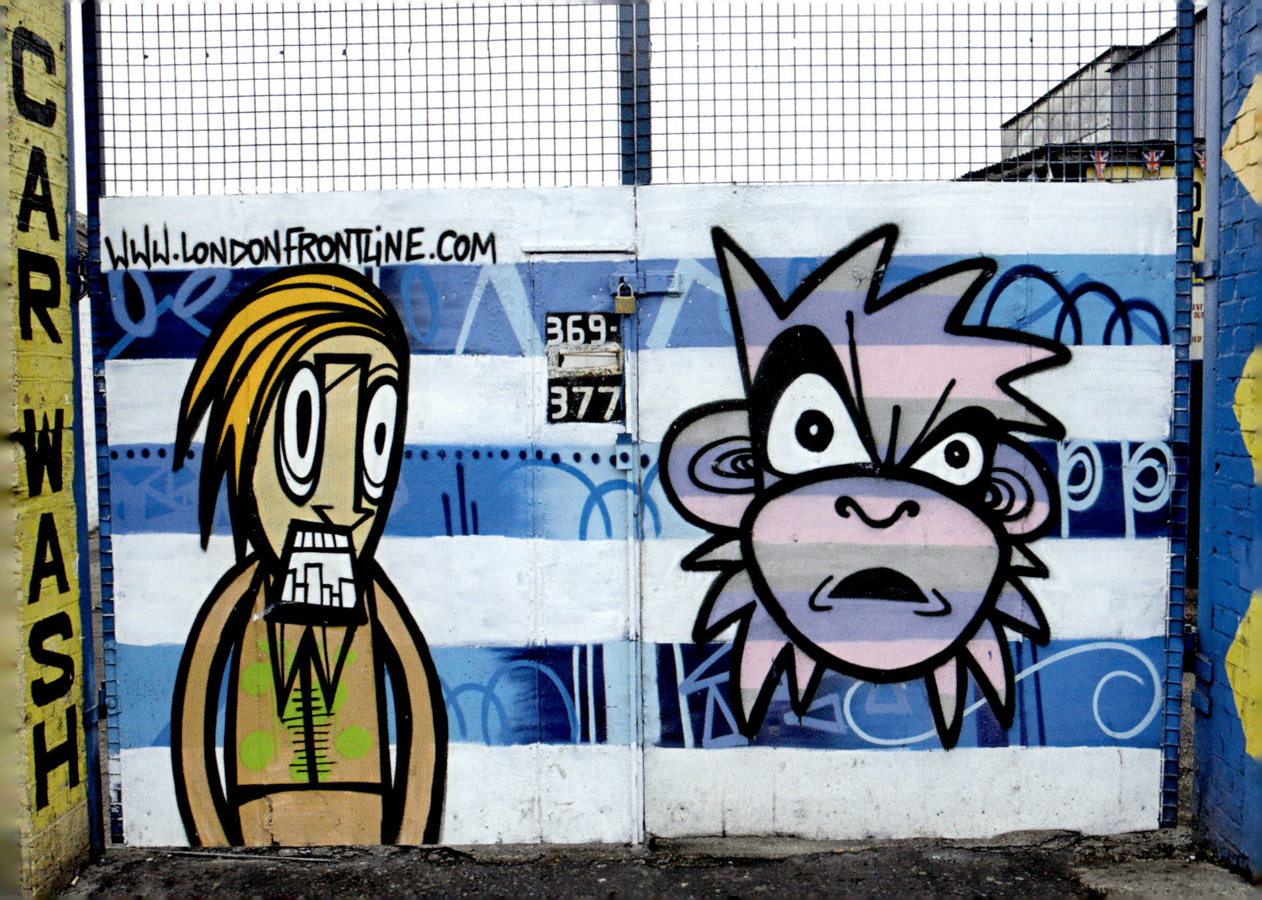
CAR WASH
WWW.LONDONFRONTLINE.COM
369-
377

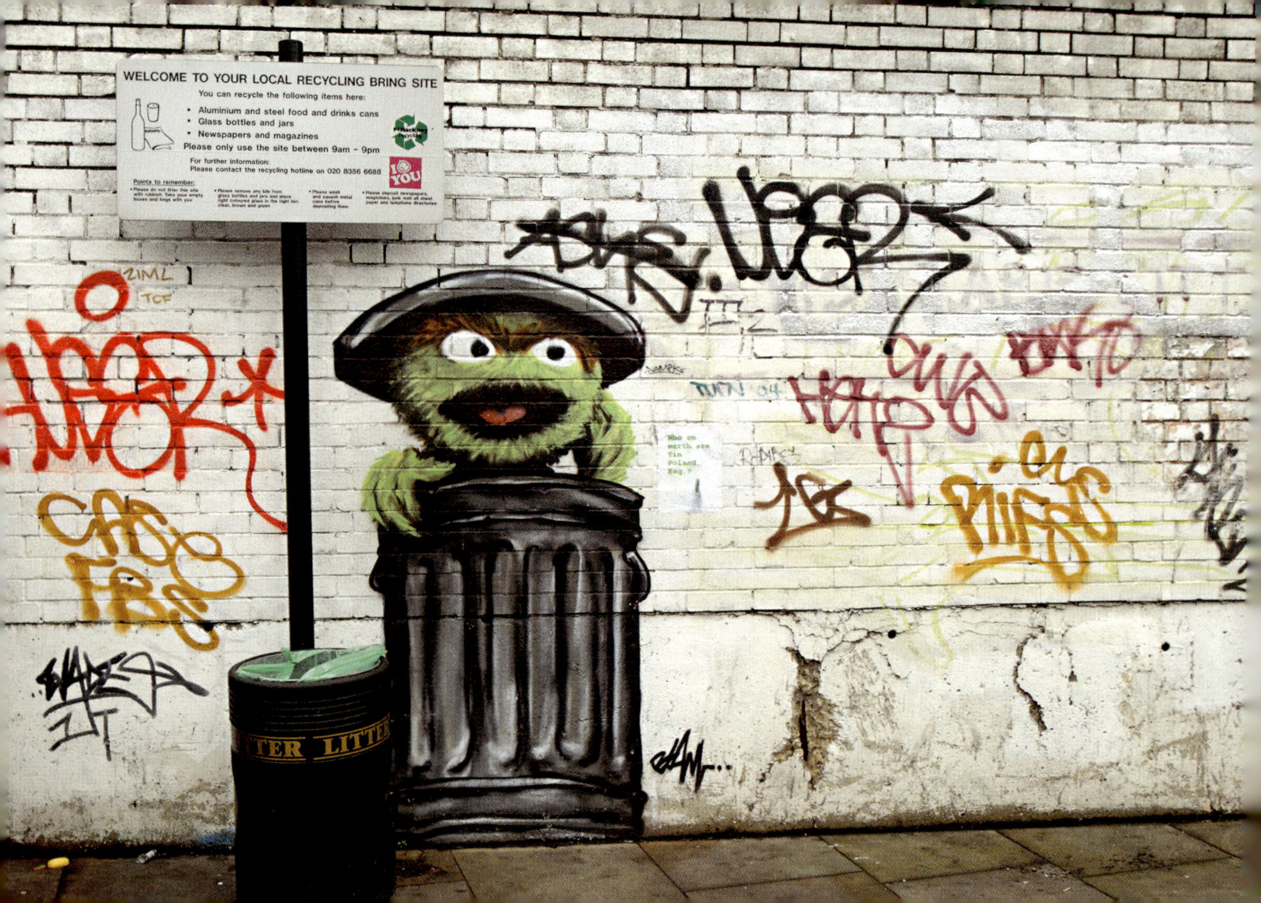
WELCOME TO YOUR LOCAL RECYCLING BRING SITE
You can recycle the following items here:
• Aluminium and steel food and drinks cans
• Glass bottles and jars
• Newspapers and magazines
Please only use the site between 9am - 9pm
For further information:
Please contact the recycling hotline on 020 8356 6688
I YOU
Points to remember:
TER LITTER

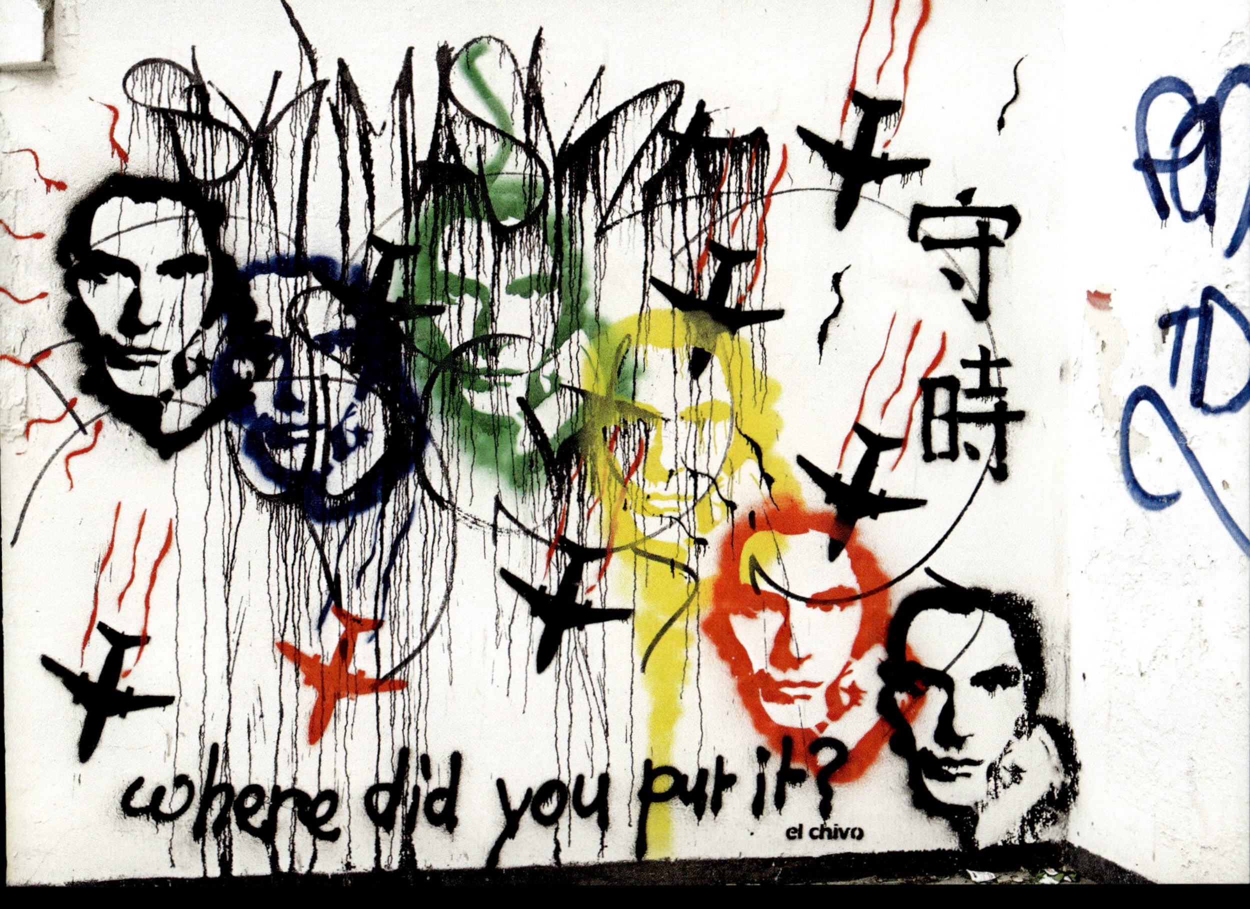

守時
where did you put it?
el chivo

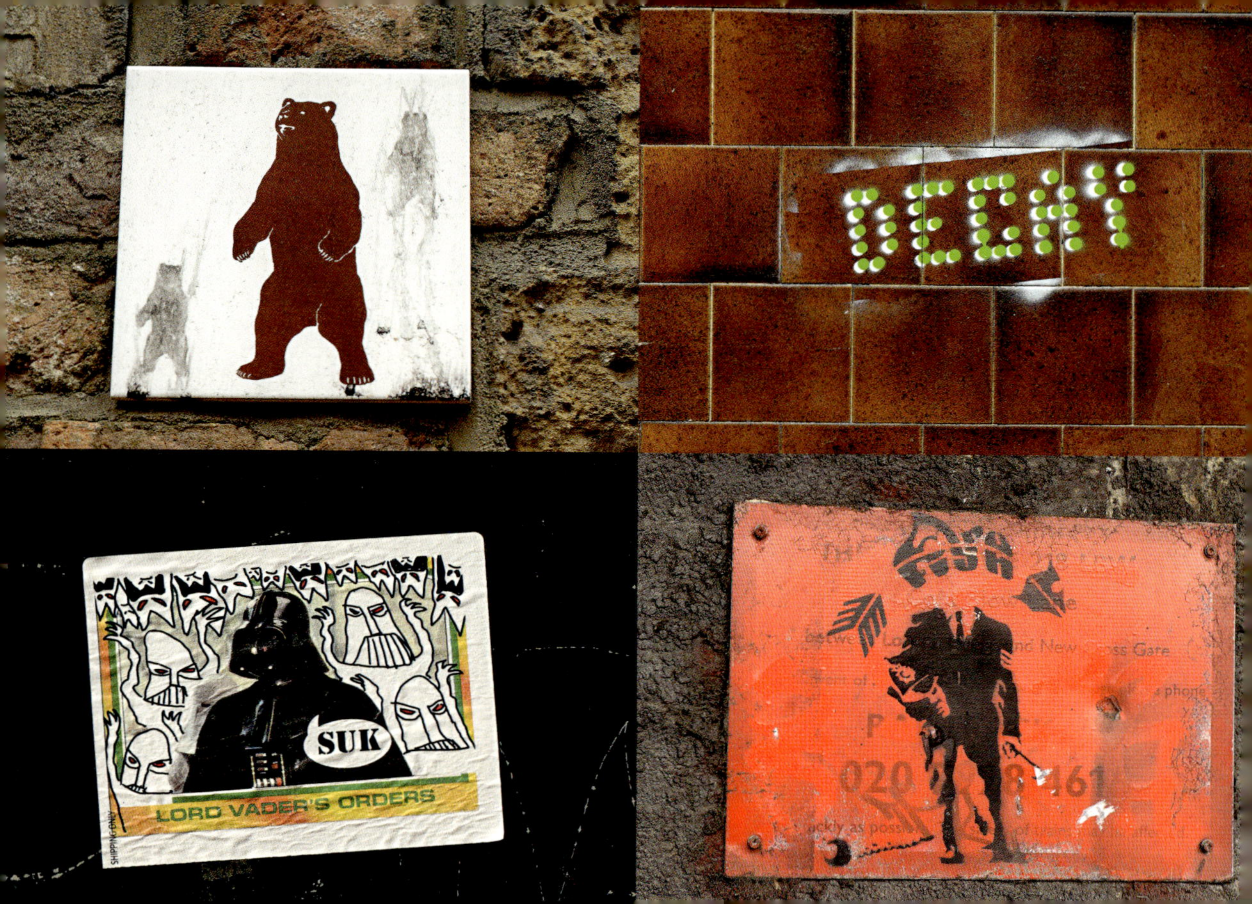
DECAY
SUK
LORD VADER'S ORDERS
New Cross Gate

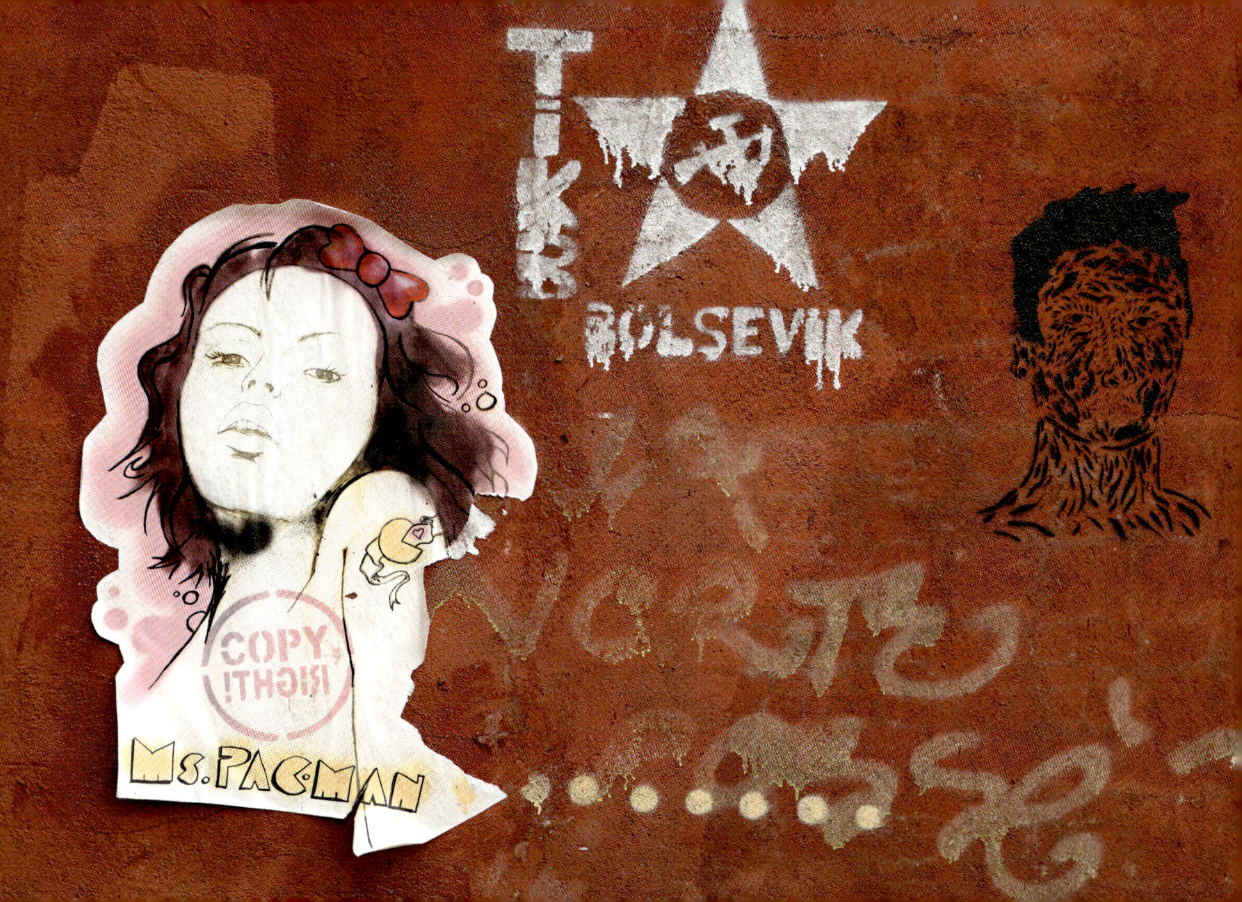
BOLSEVIK
COPY
Ms.PACMAN

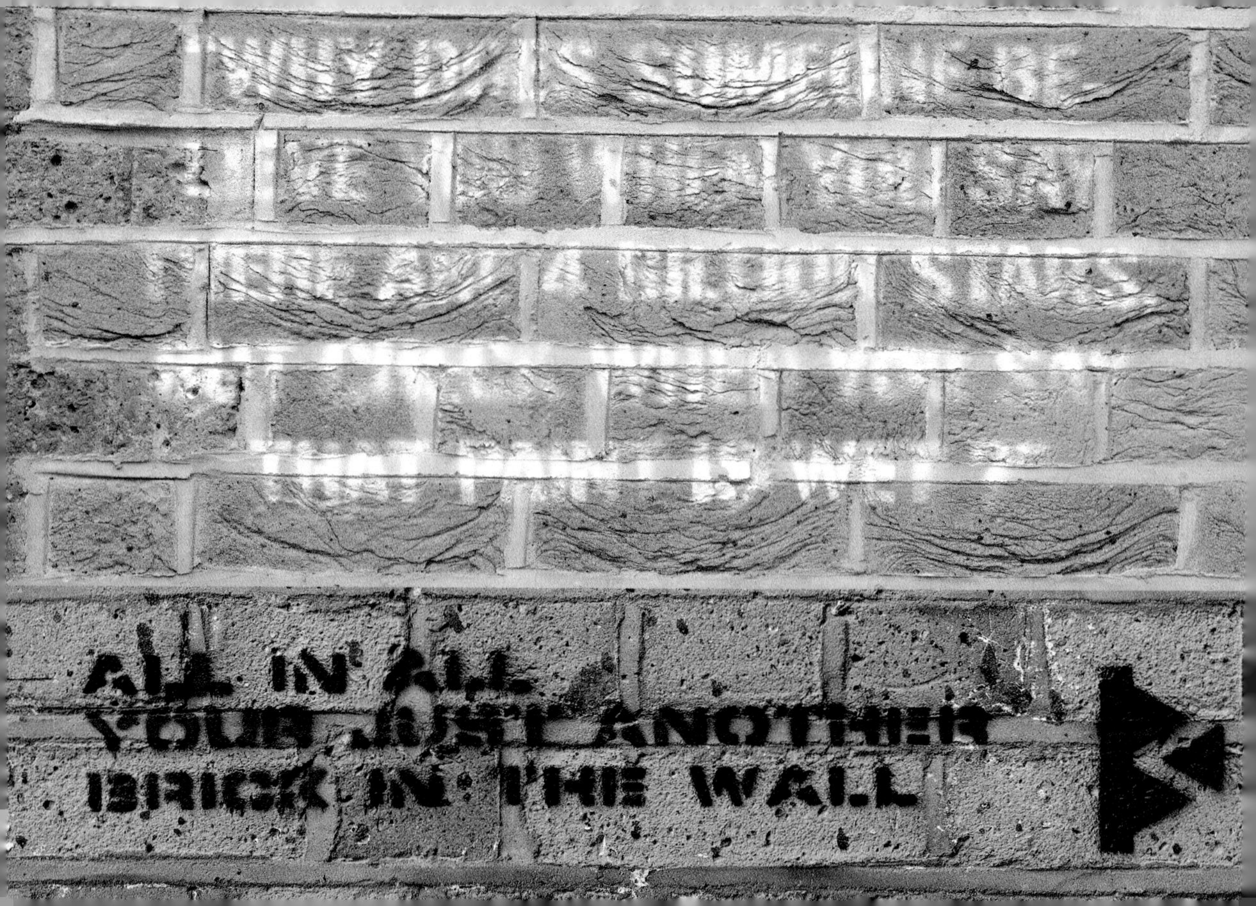
ALL IN ALL
YOUR JUST ANOTHER
BRICK IN THE WALL

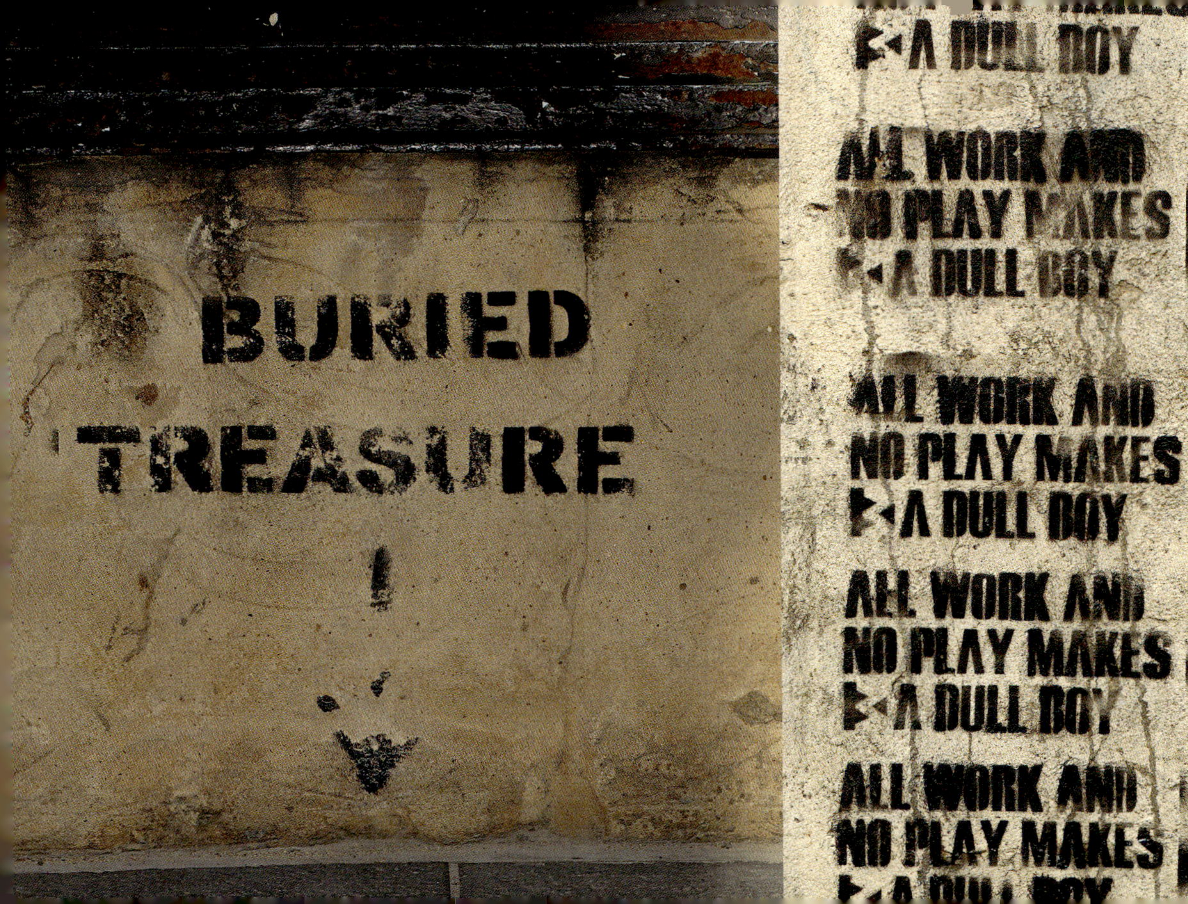
BURIED
TREASURE
A DULL BOY
ALL WORK AND
NO PLAY MAKES
A DULL BOY
ALL WORK AND
NO PLAY MAKES
A DULL BOY
ALL WORK AND
NO PLAY MAKES
A DULL BOY
ALL WORK AND
NO PLAY MAKES

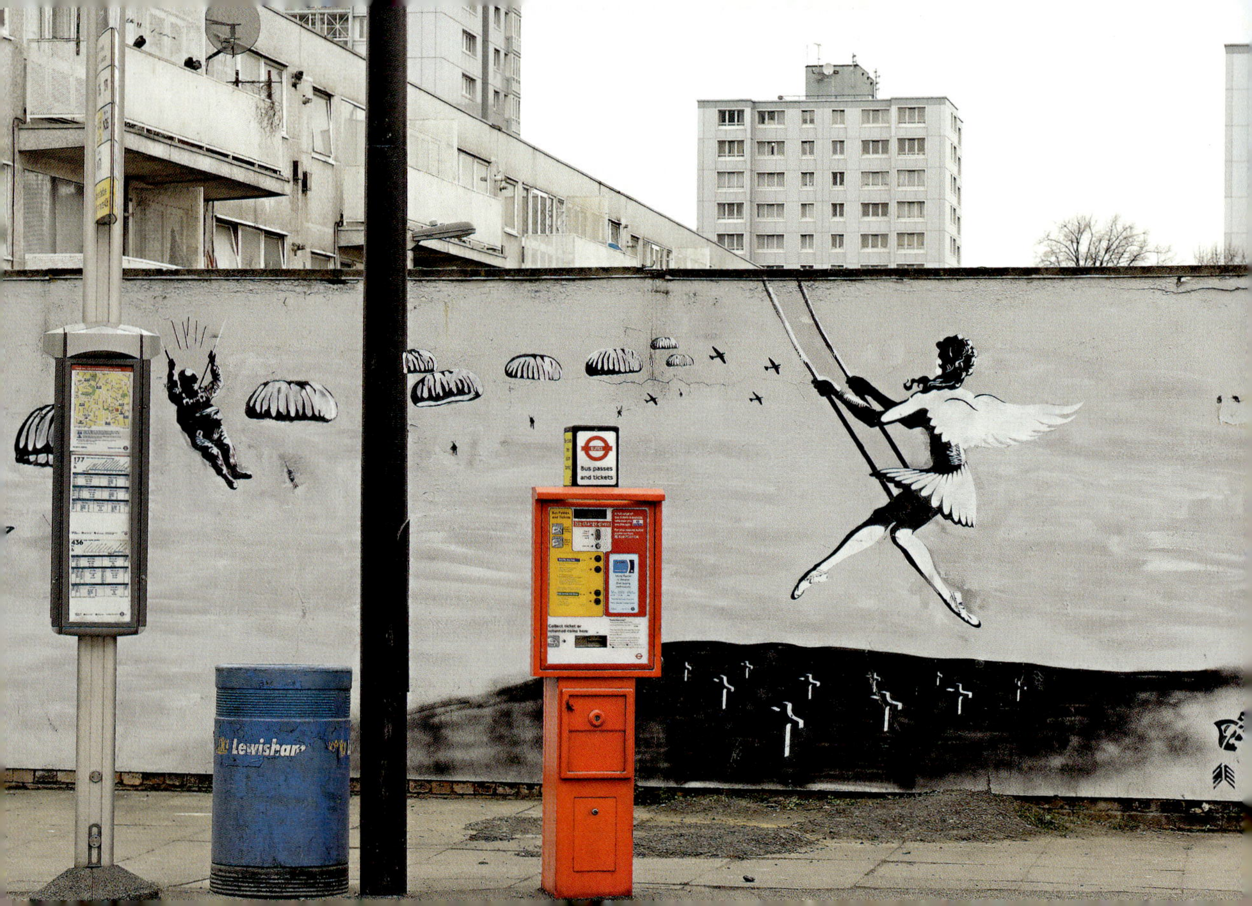
Bus passes and tickets
Lewisham

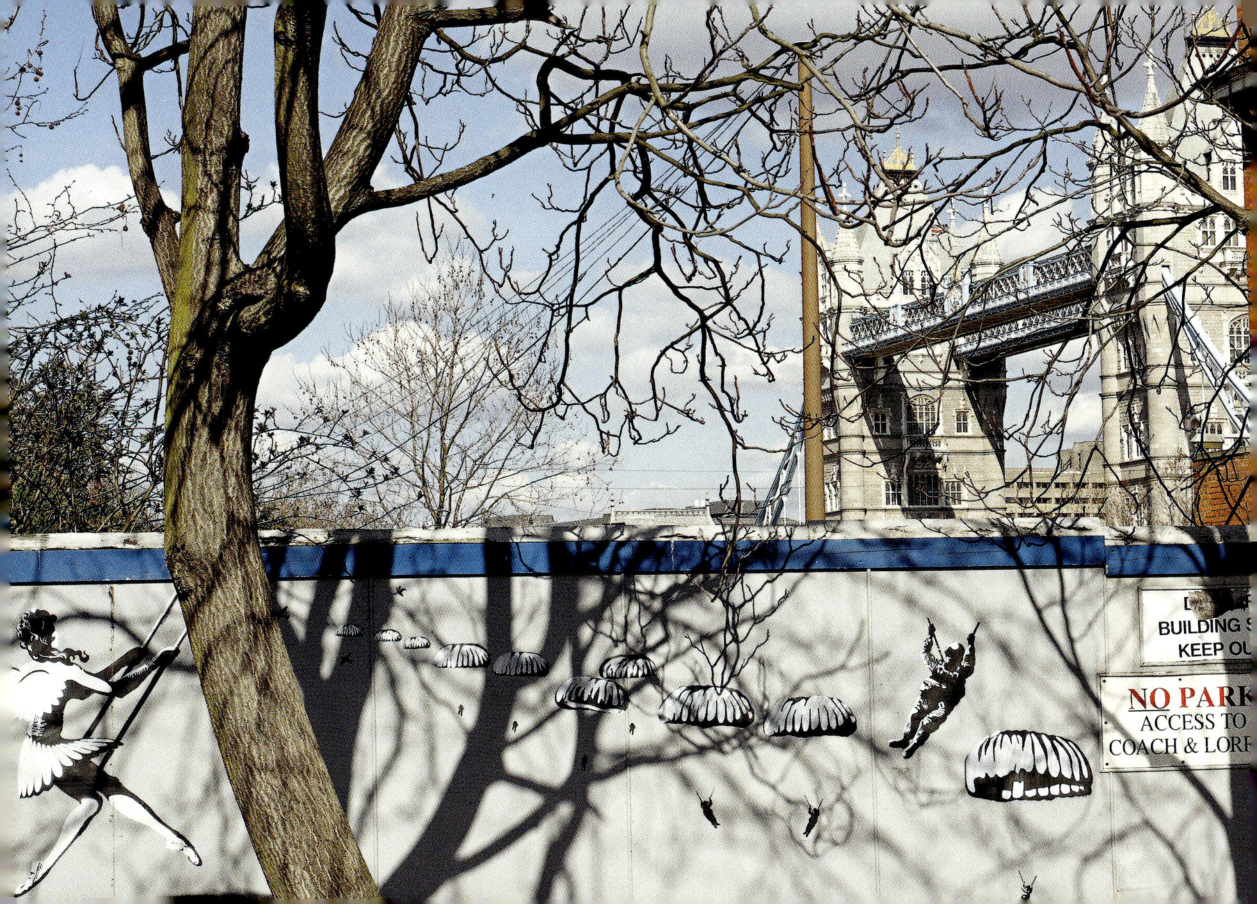
BUILDING S
KEEP OU
NO PARK
ACCESS TO
COACH & LORR

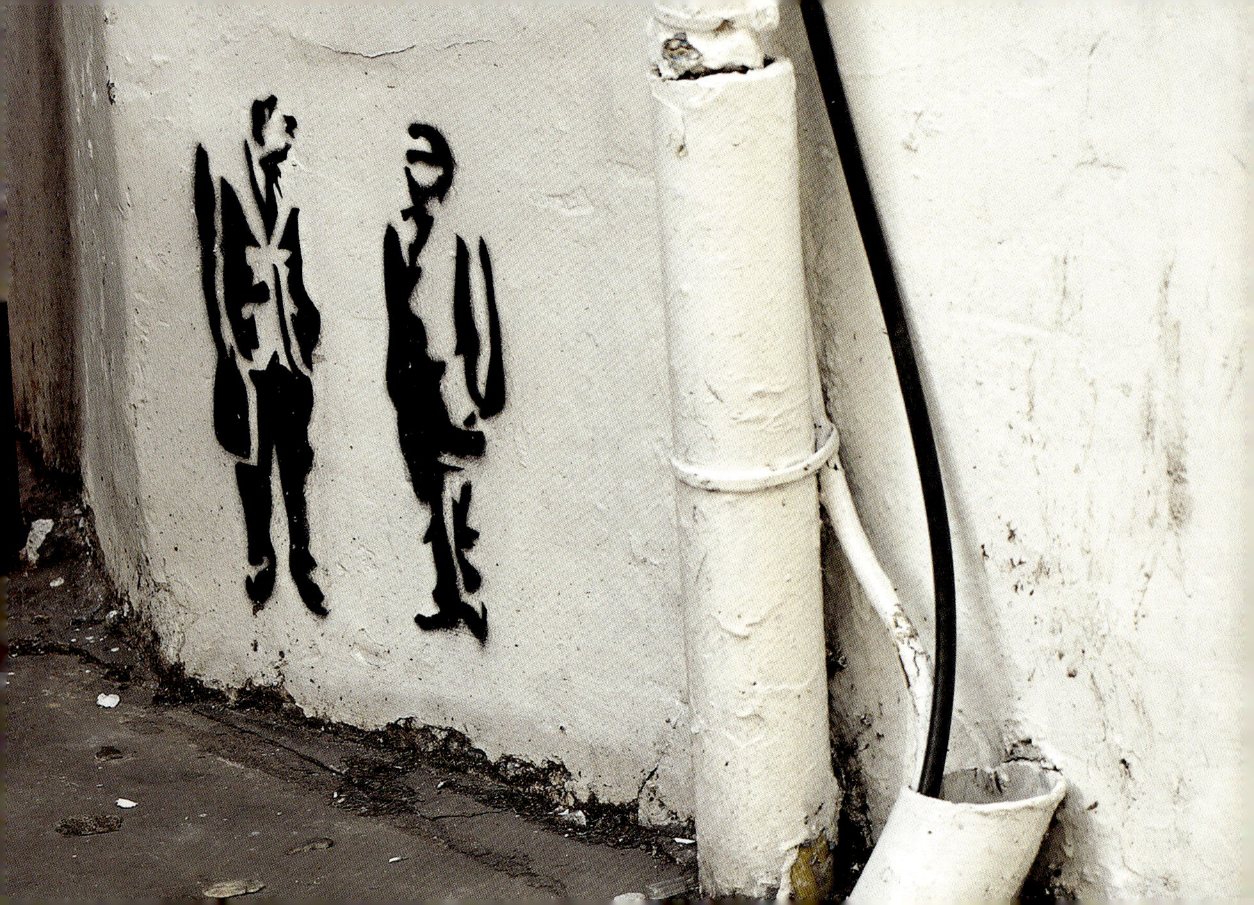

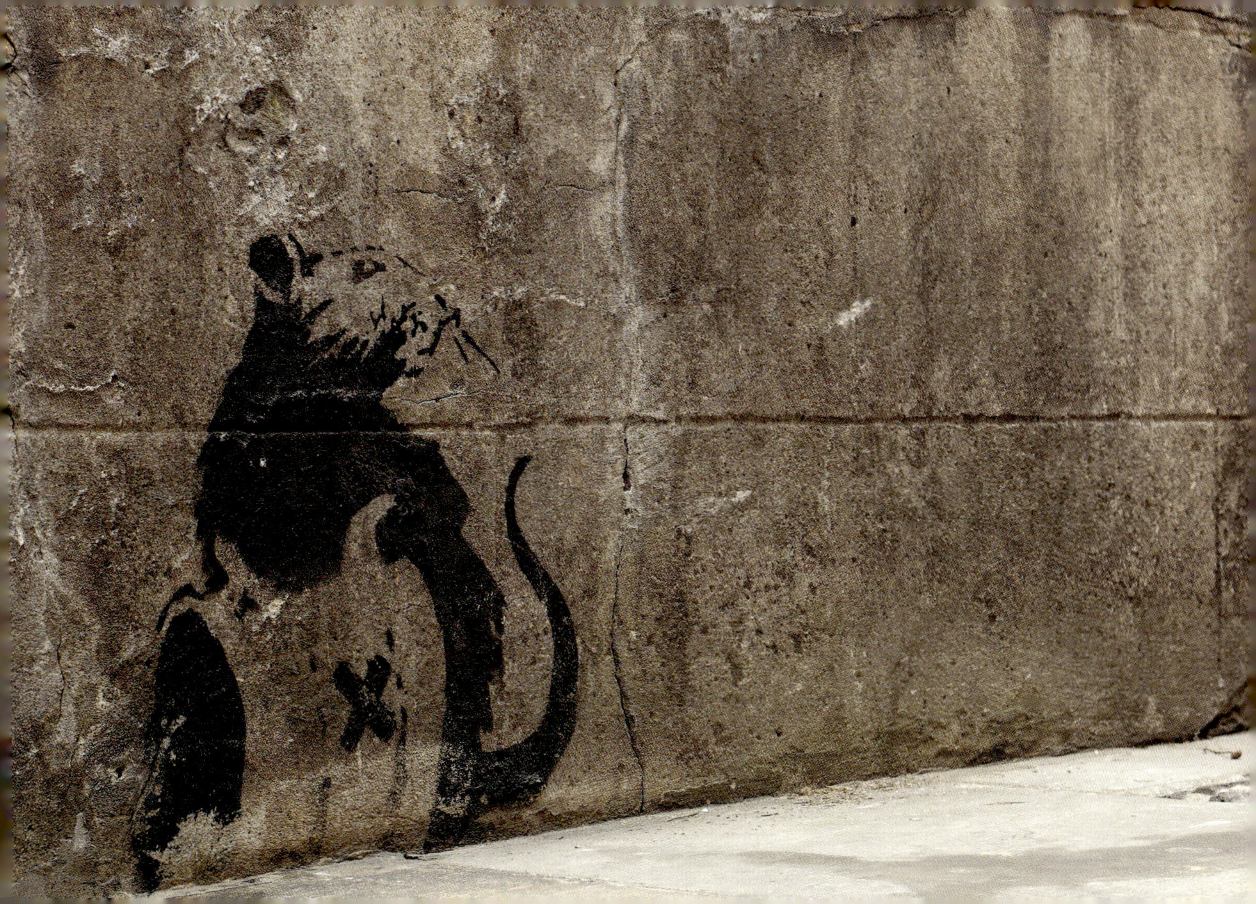

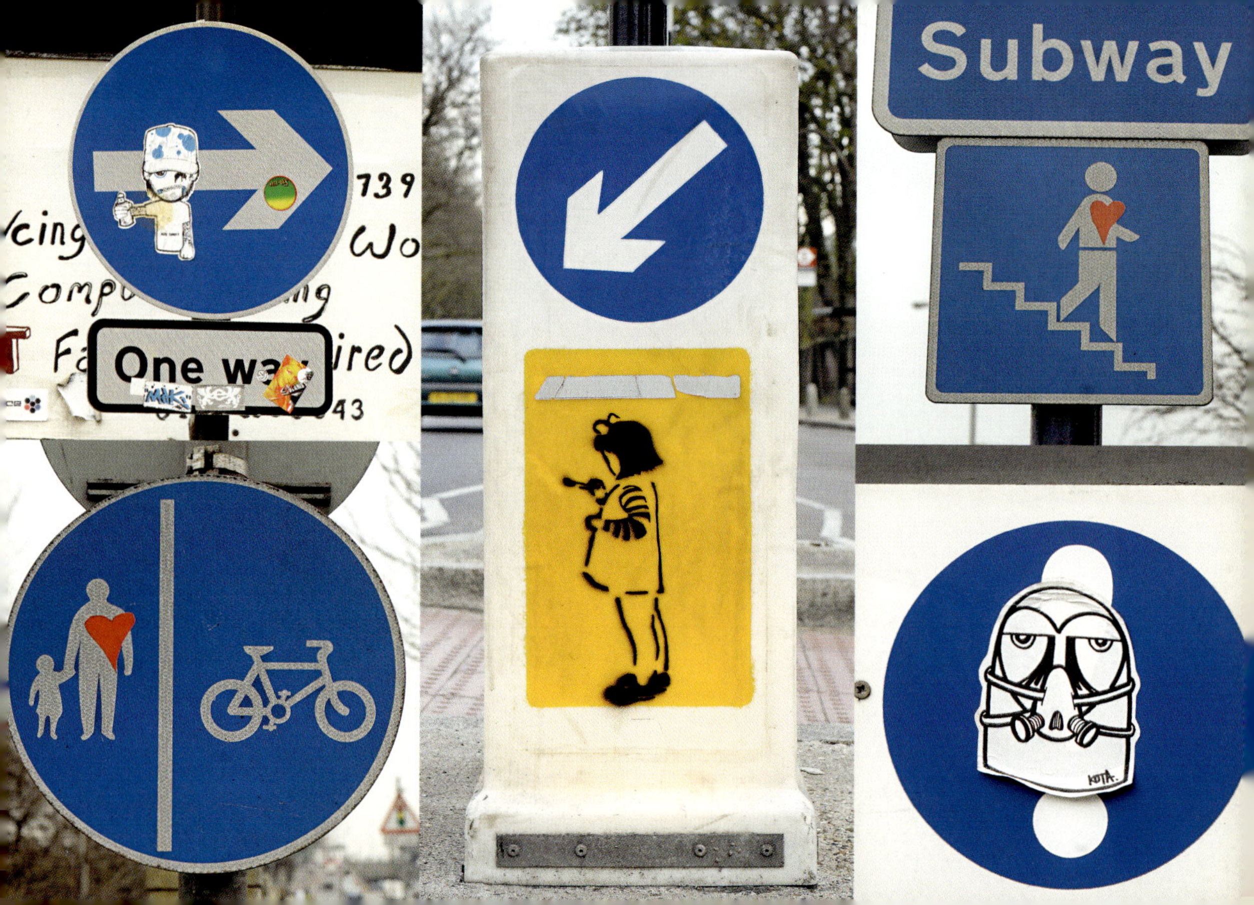

739
One way
Subway
KOTA.

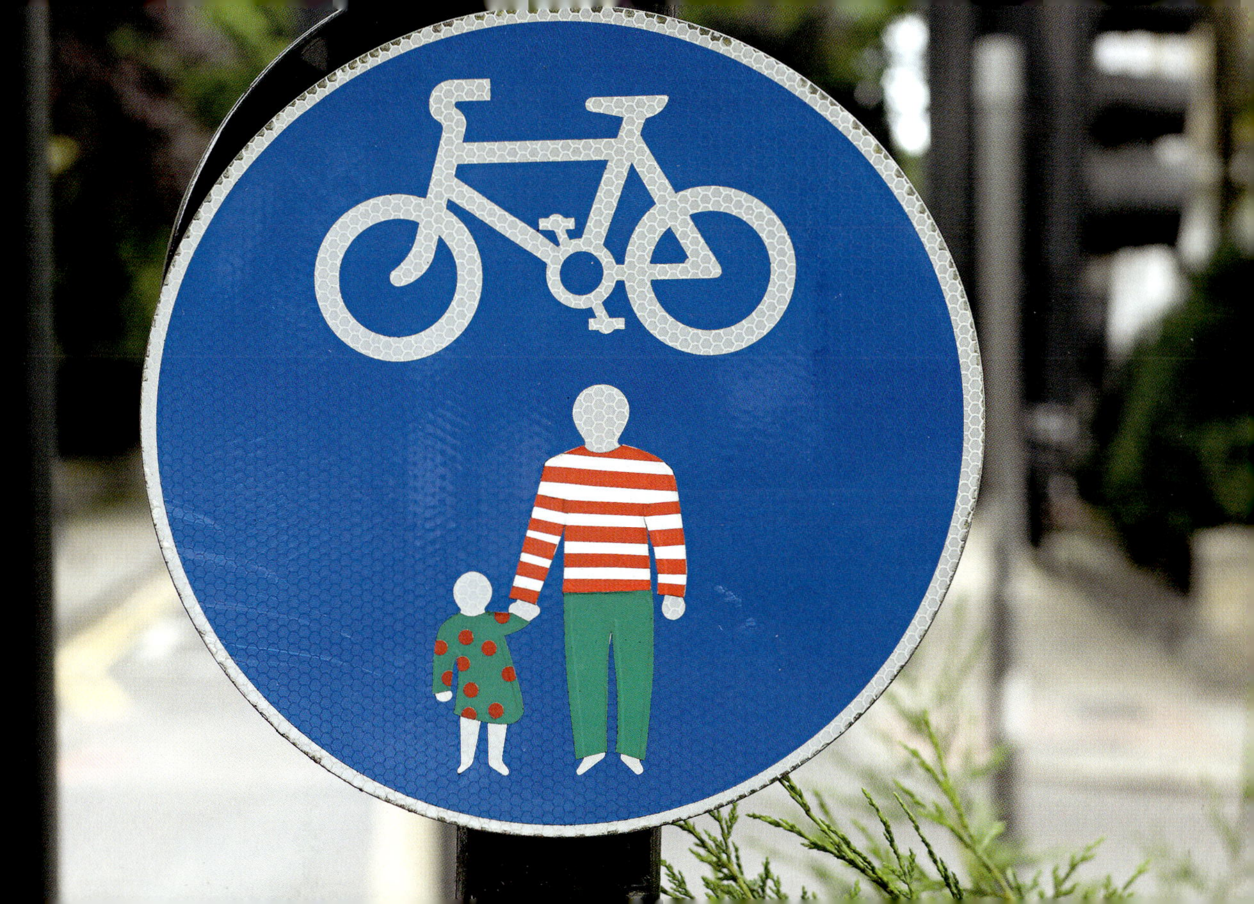

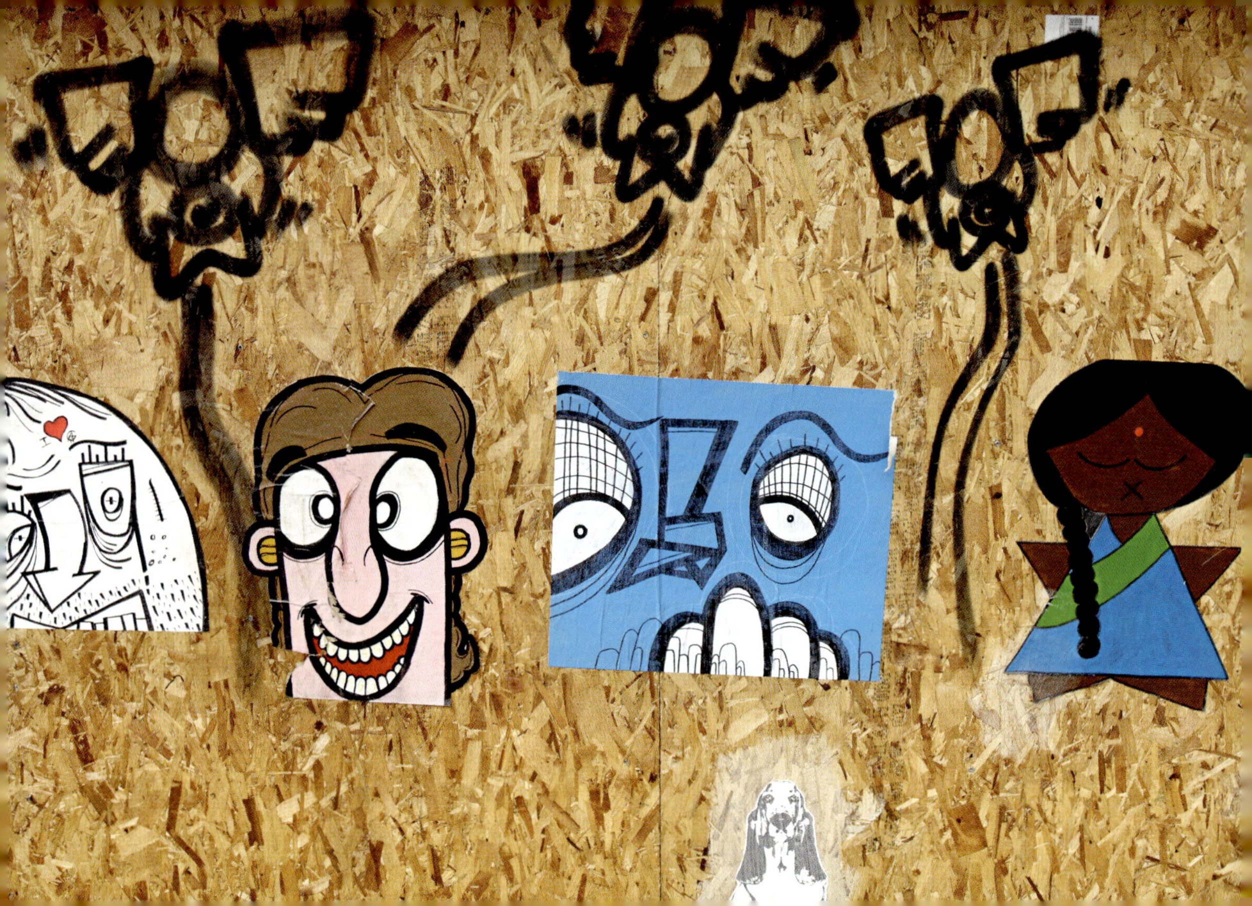

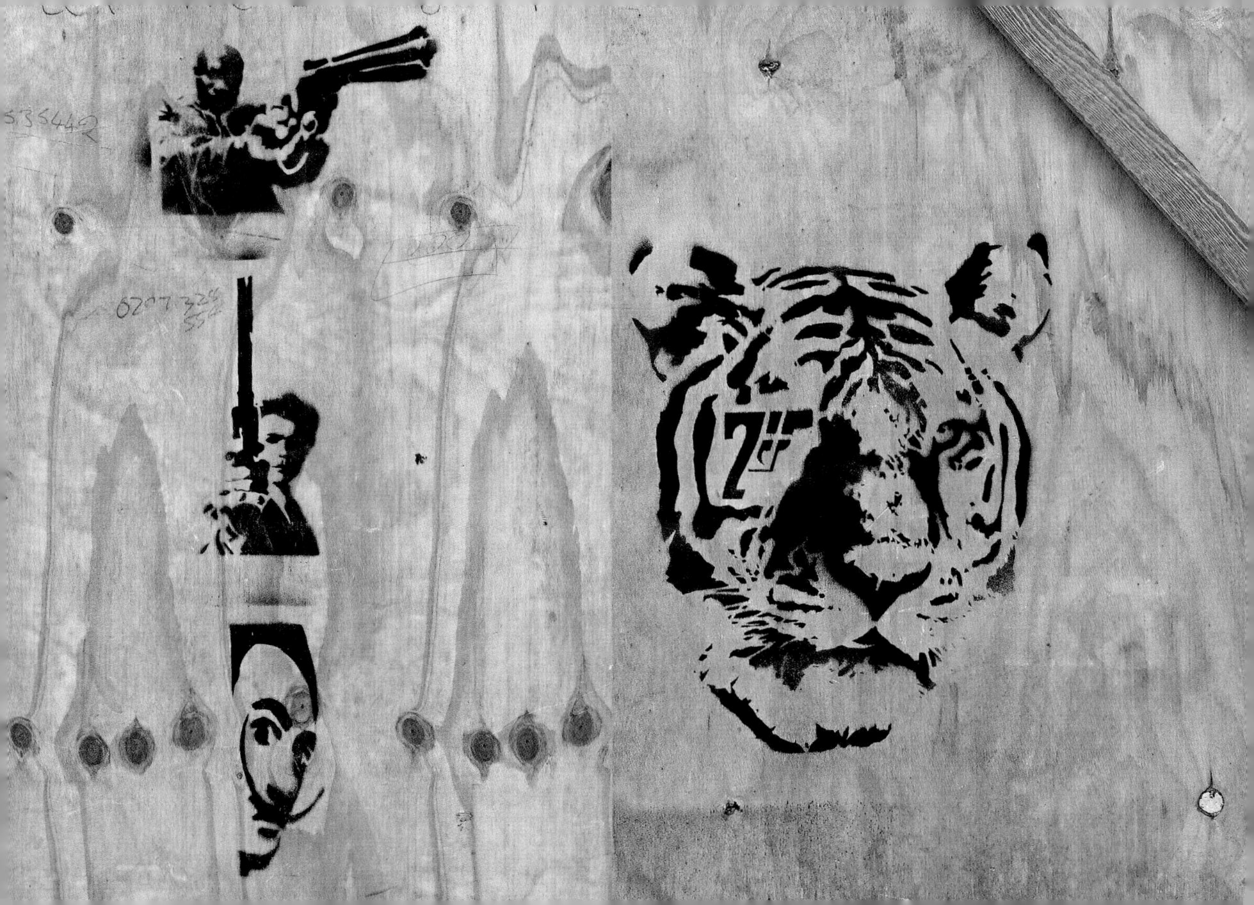

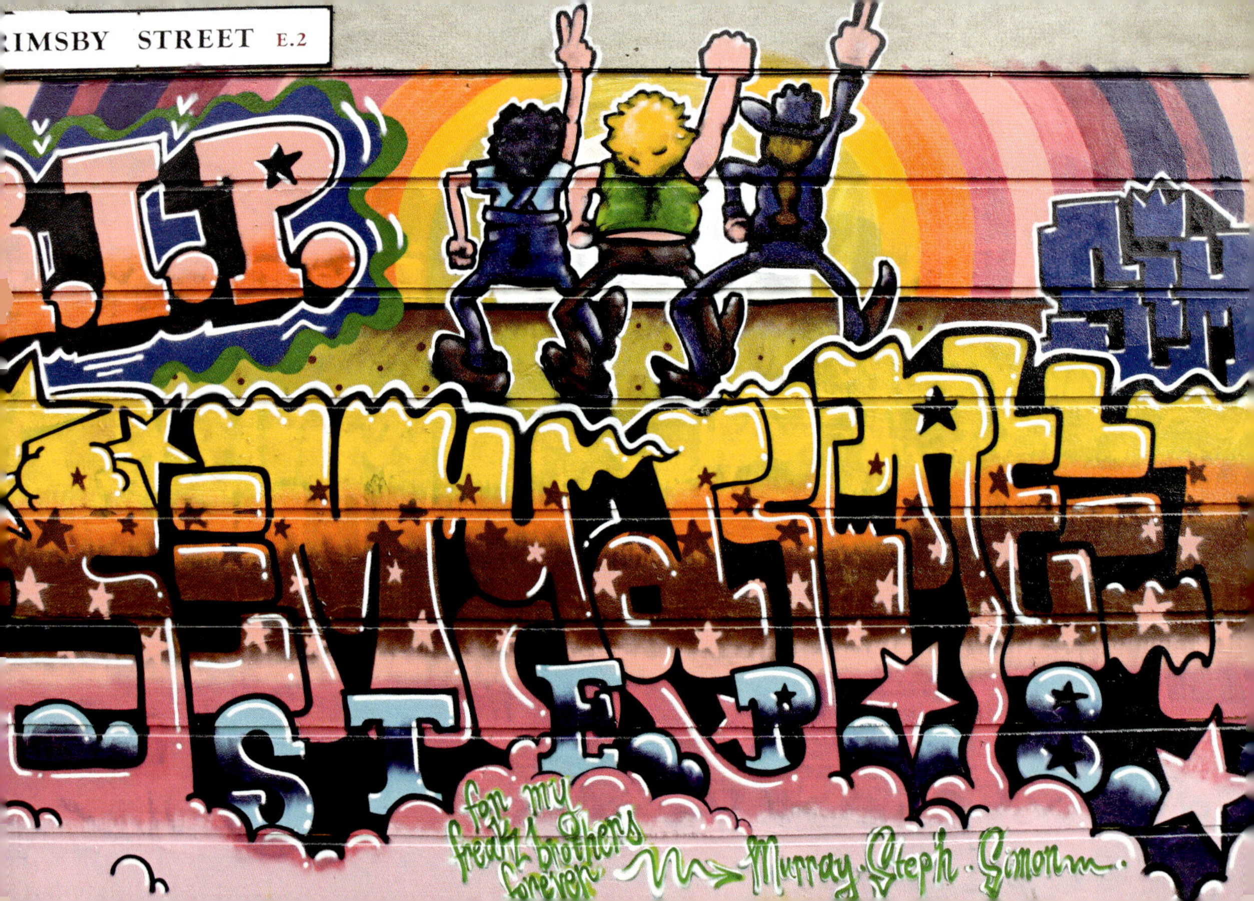

IMSBY STREET E.2
for my freak brothers forever
Murray . Steph . Simon

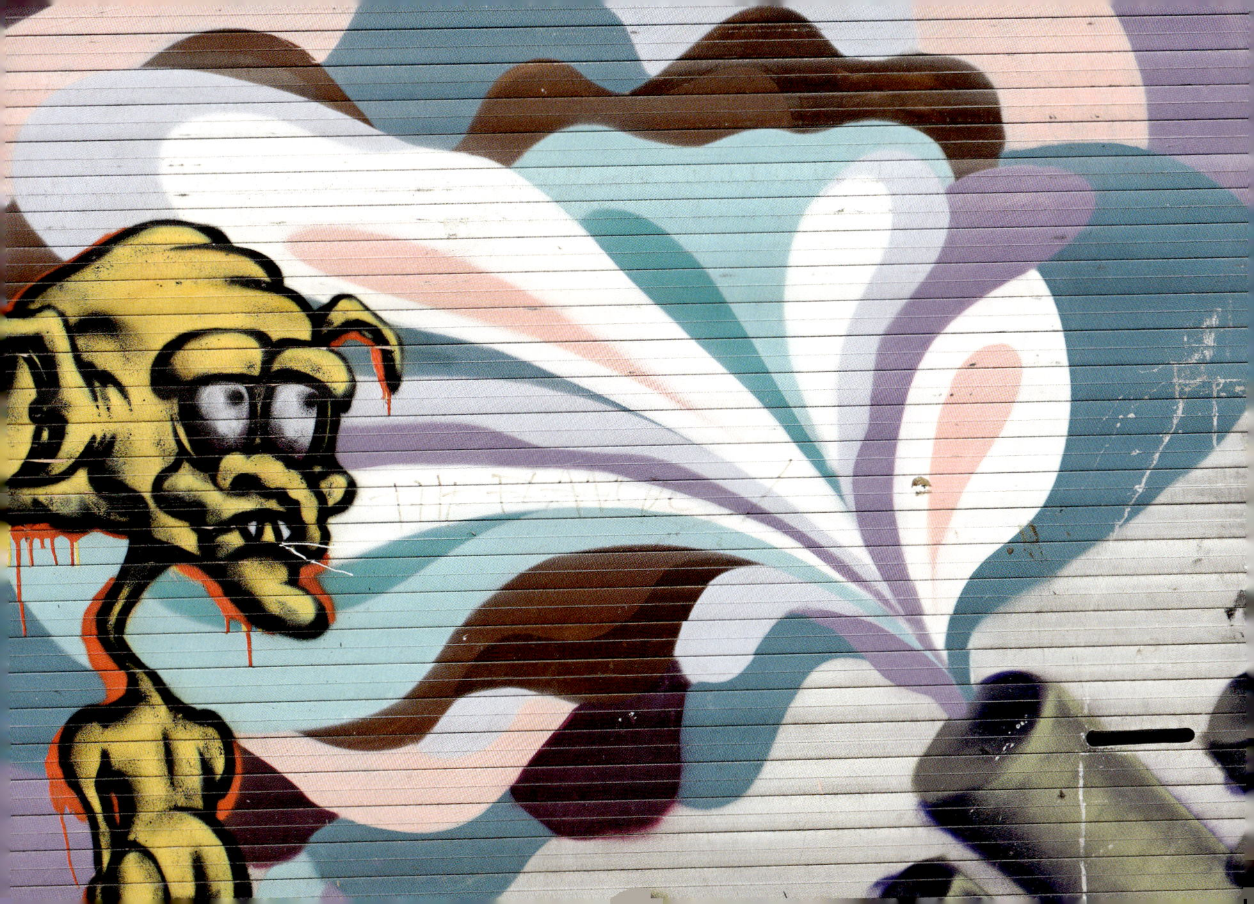

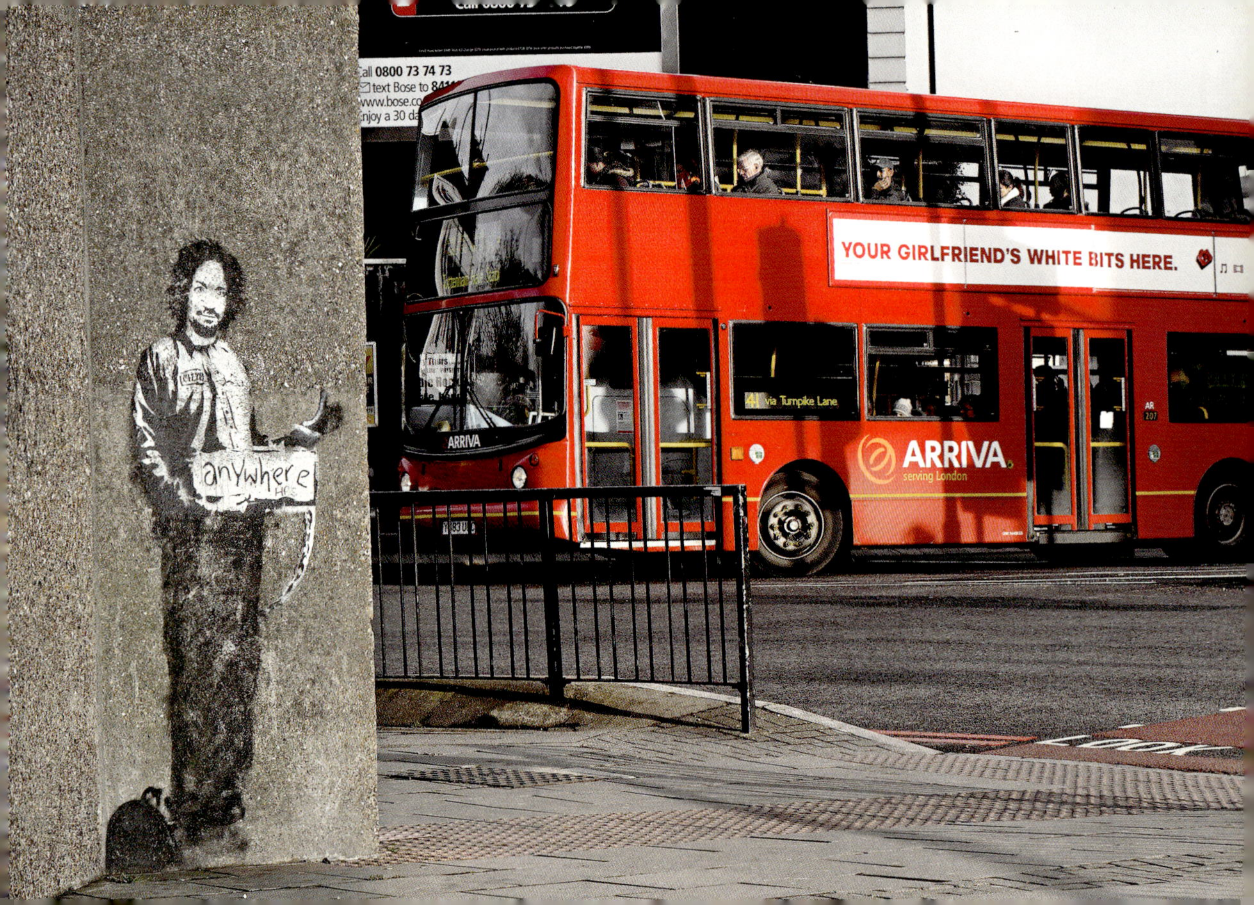
anywhere
Call 0800 73 74 73
YOUR GIRLFRIEND'S WHITE BITS HERE.
41 via Turnpike Lane
ARRIVA
ARRIVA
serving London

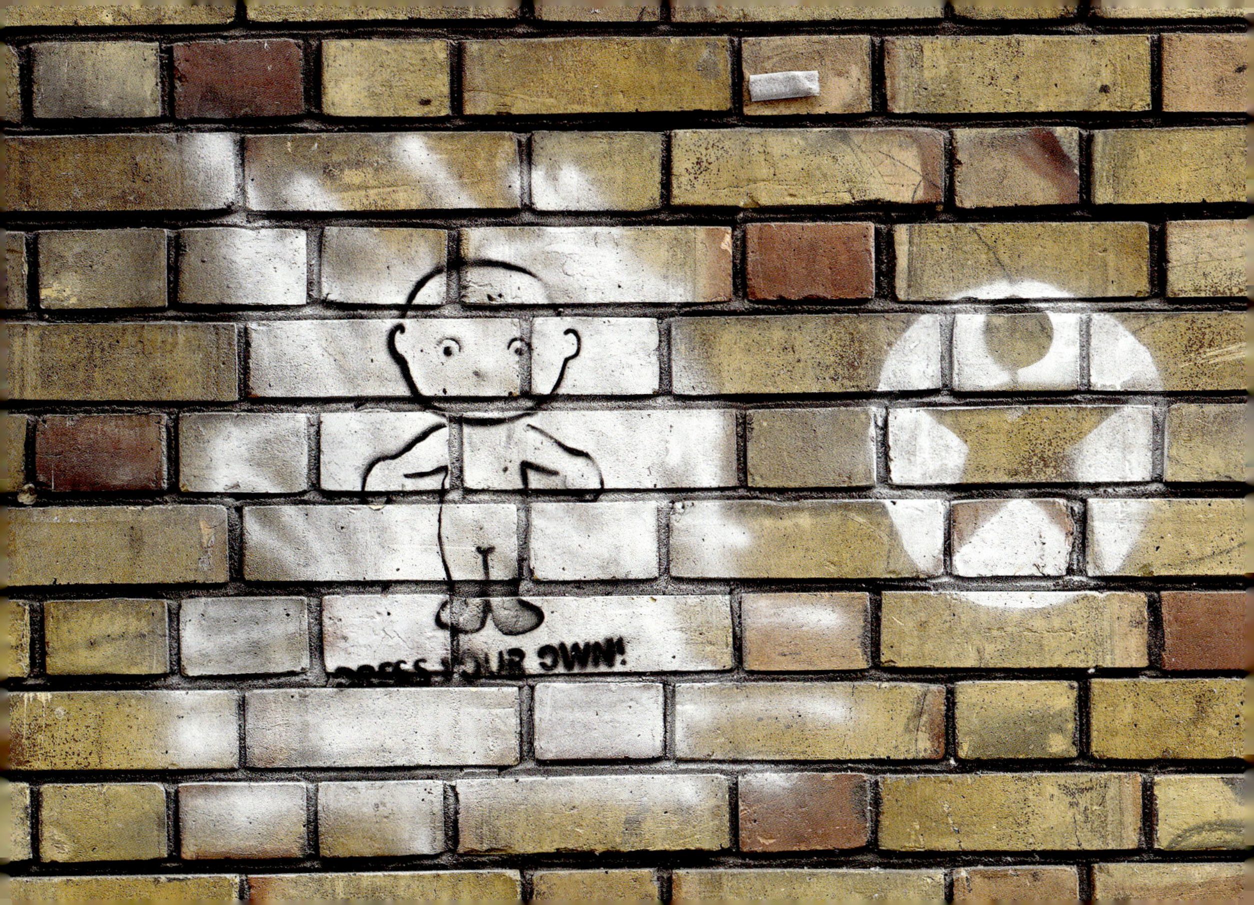
OWN!

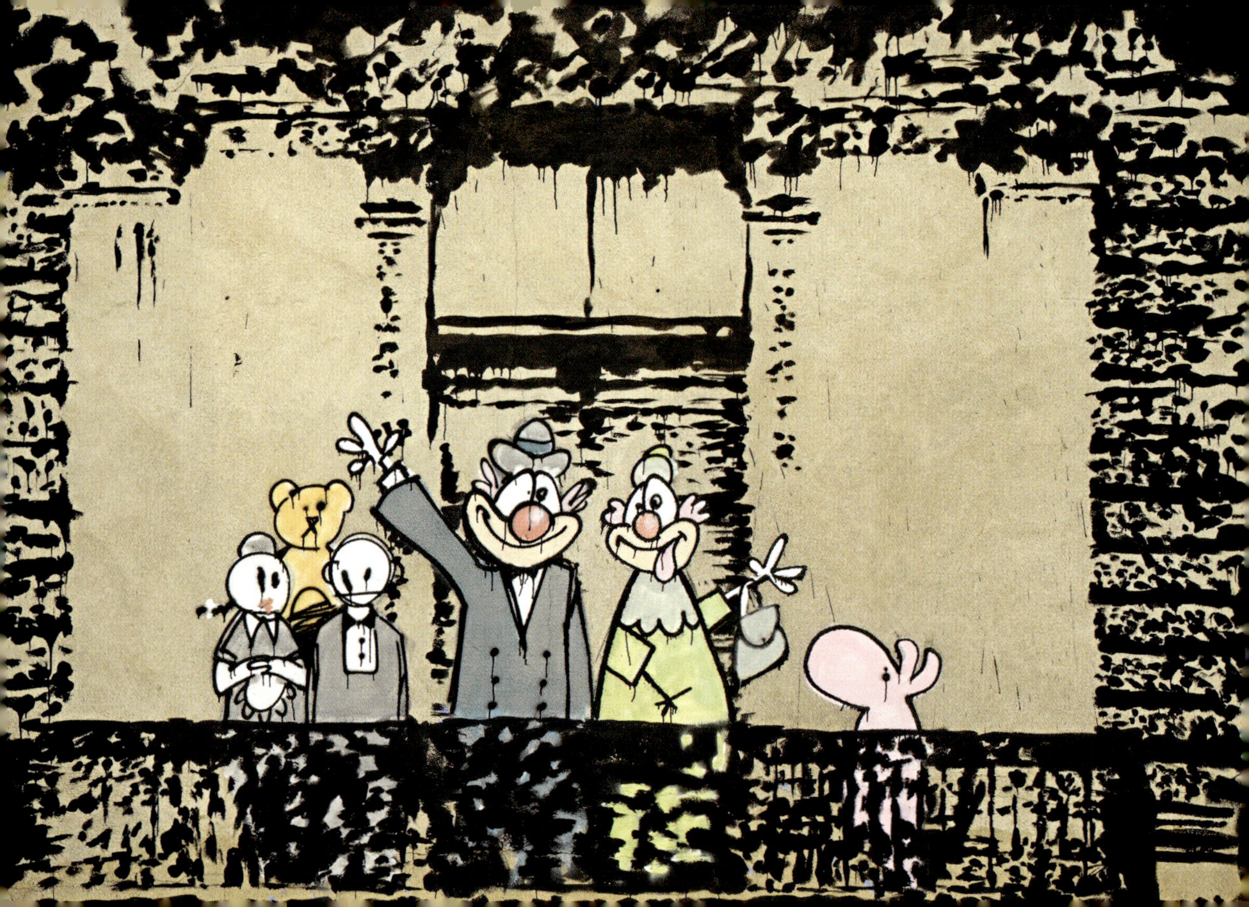

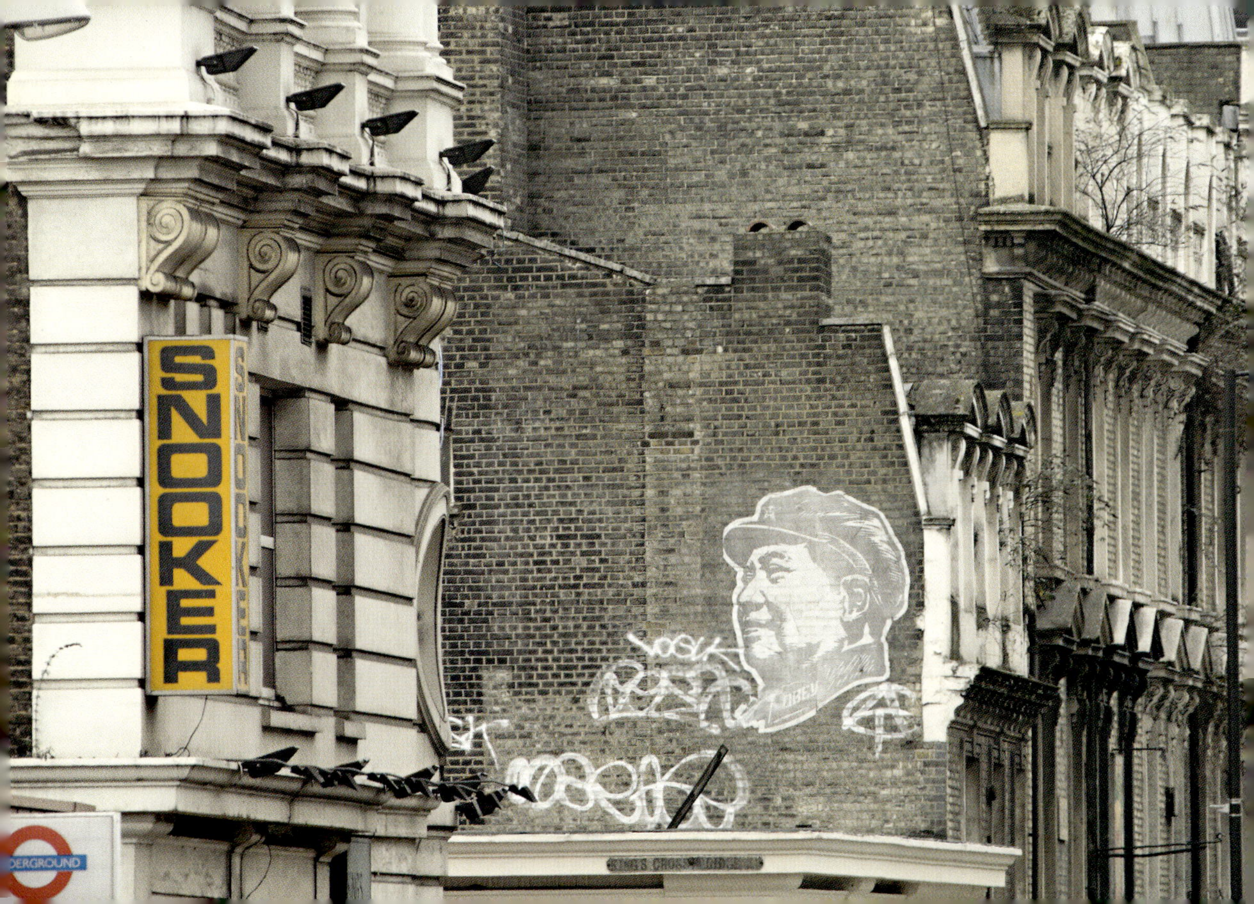
SNOOKER
DERGROUND

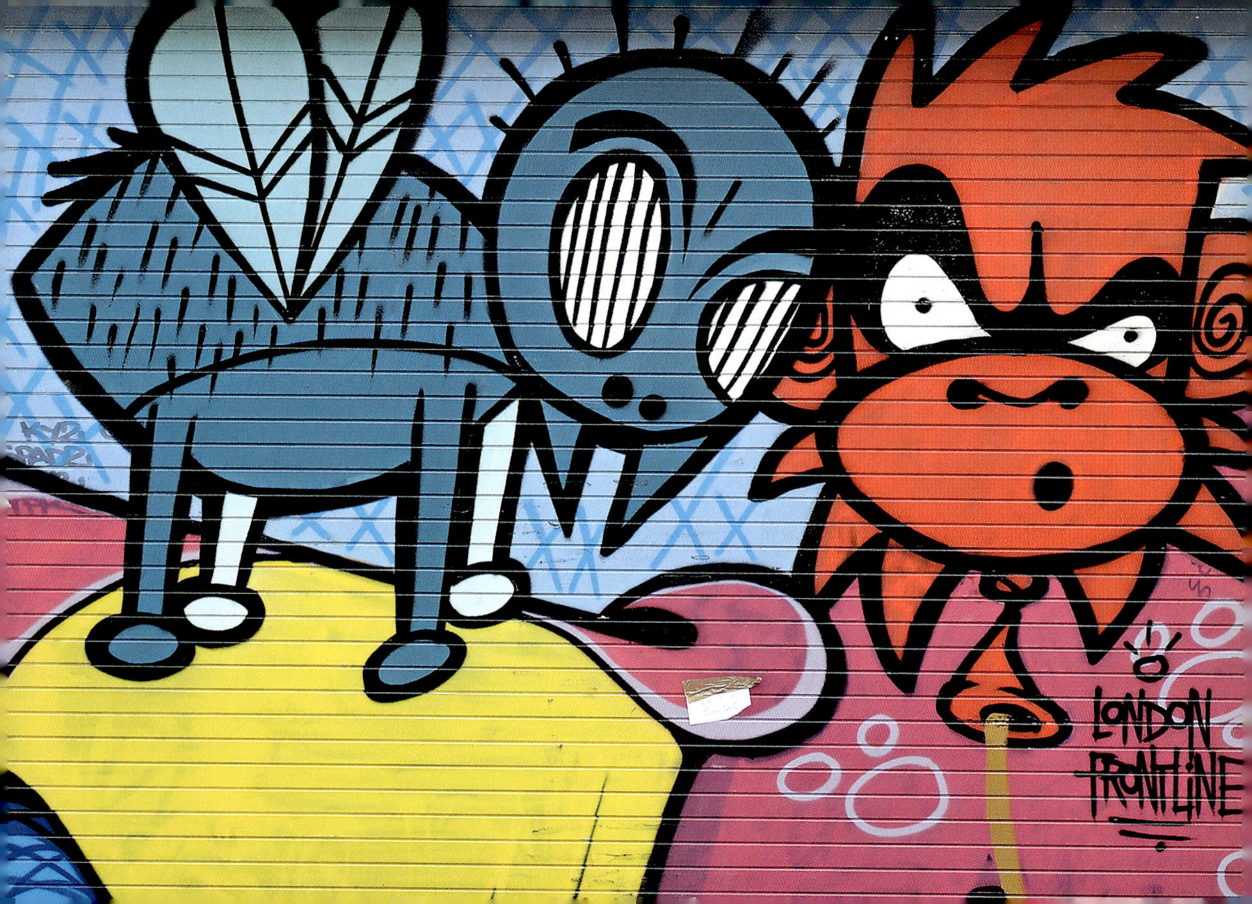
LONDON
FRONTLINE

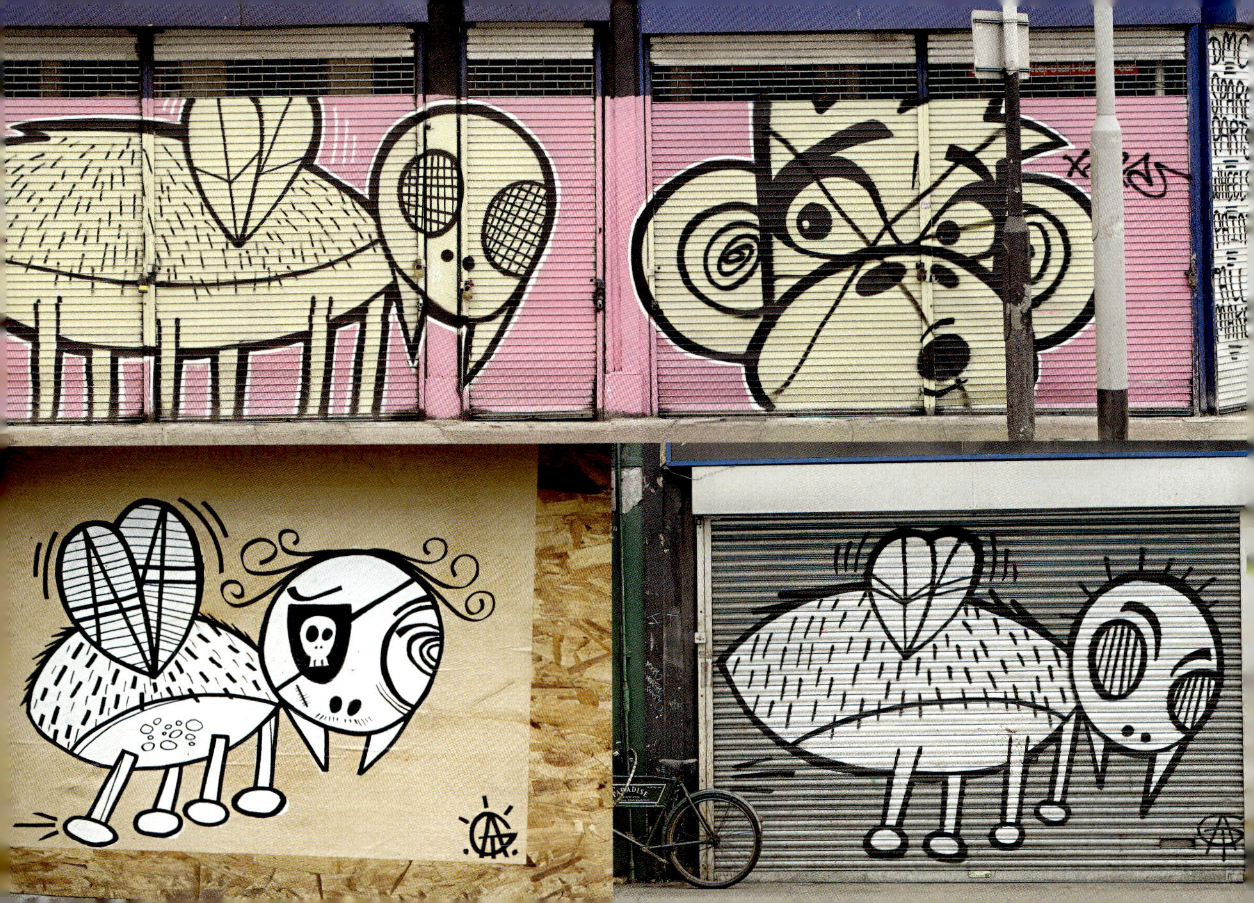
DMC
ALL
PARADISE

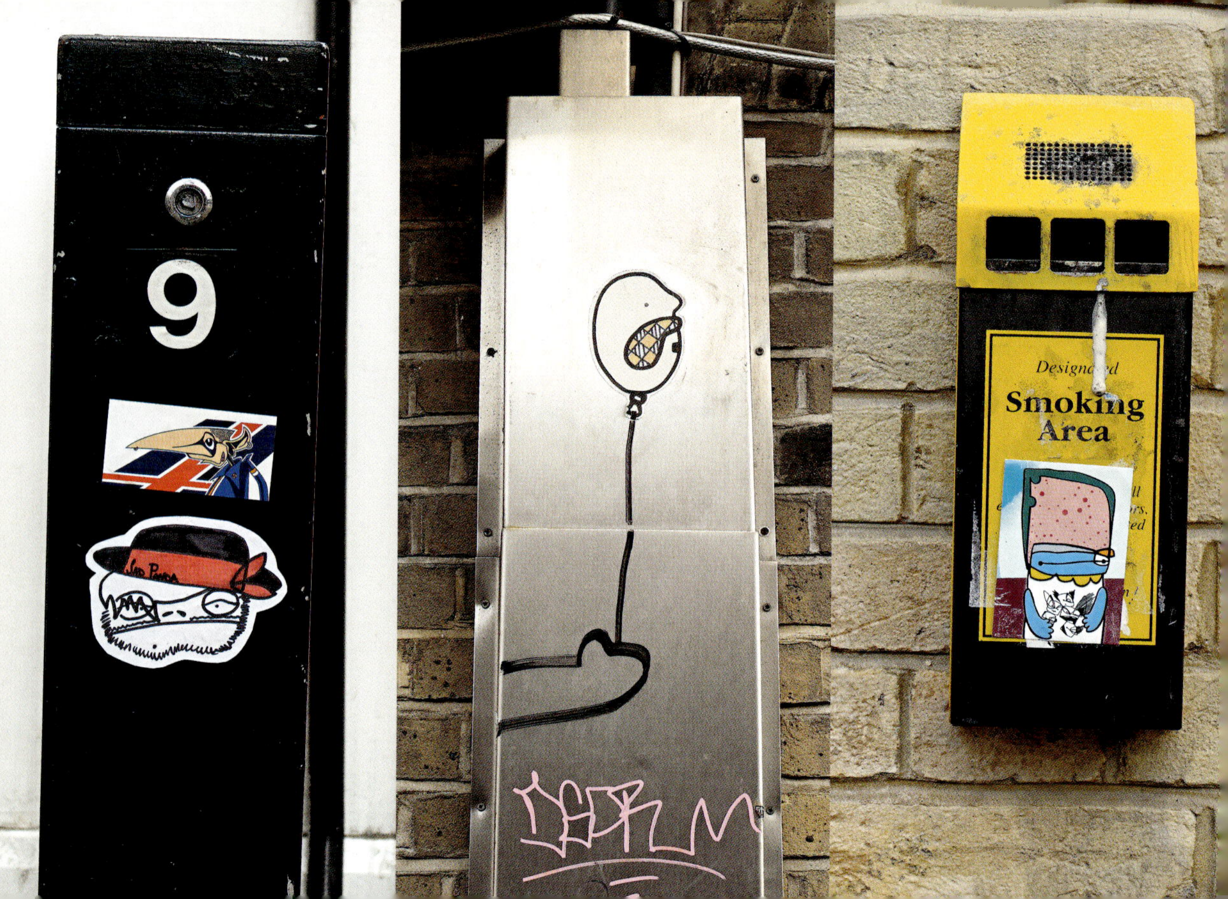
9
Smoking
Area

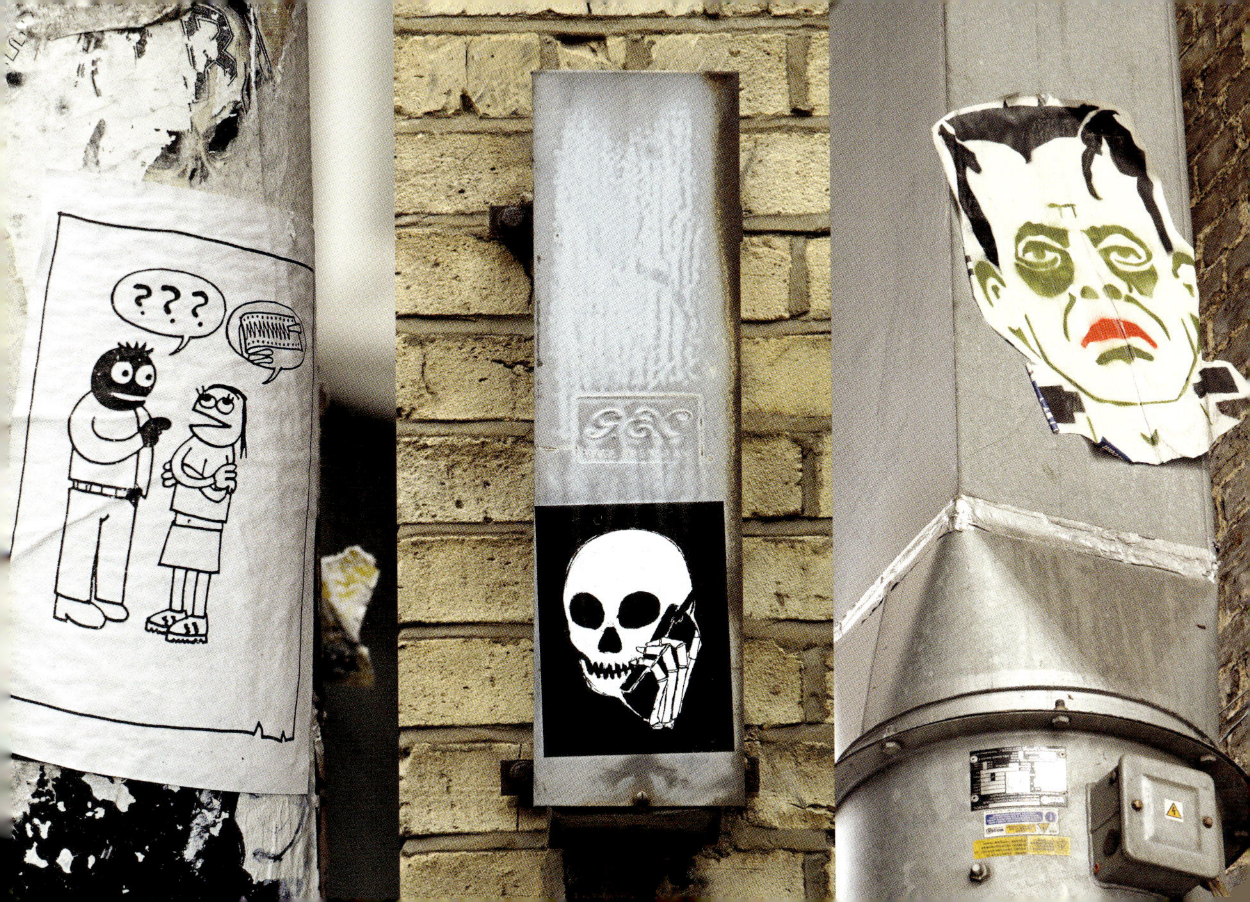
???
GEC

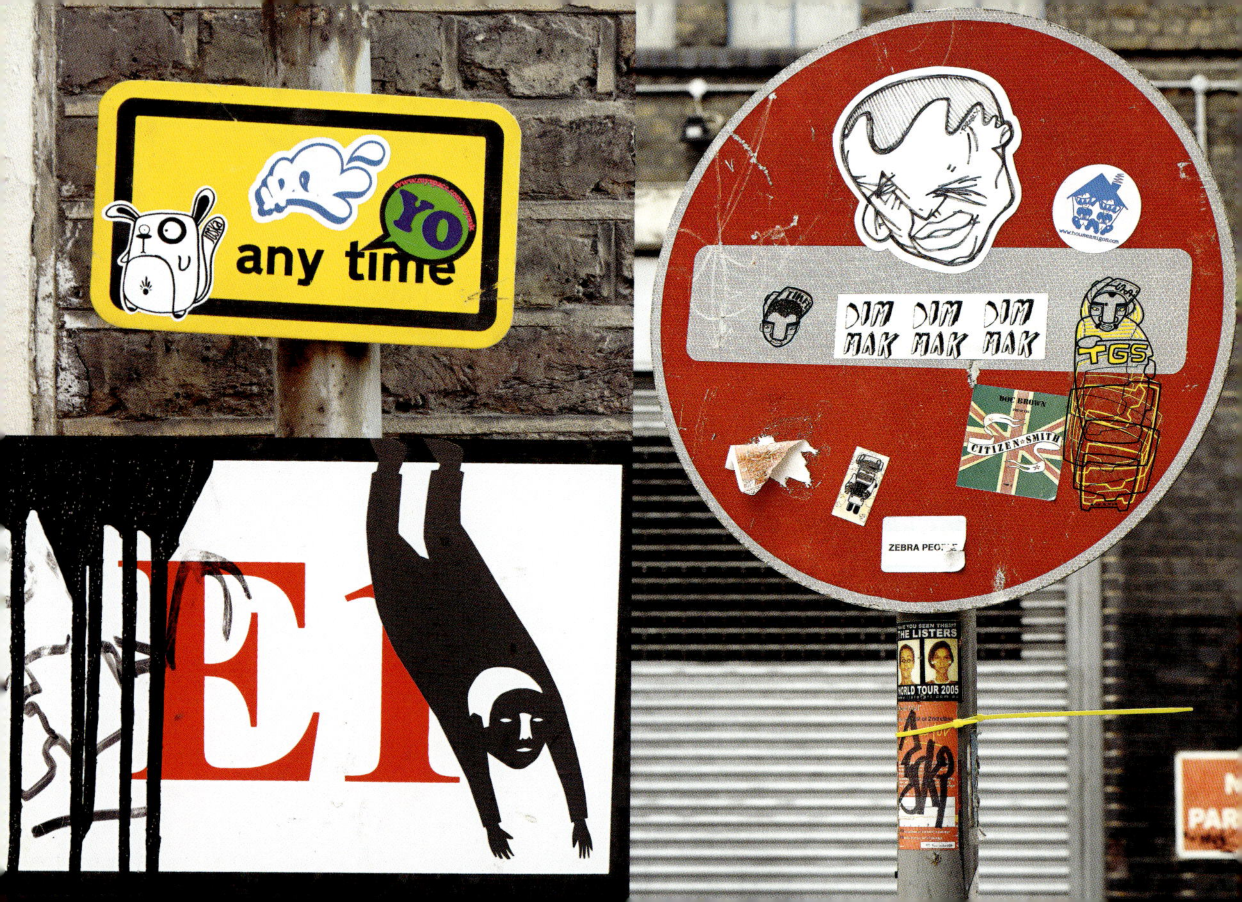
any time
YO
DIM DIM DIM
MAK MAK MAK
TGS
DOC BROWN
CITIZEN SMITH
THE LISTERS
E1

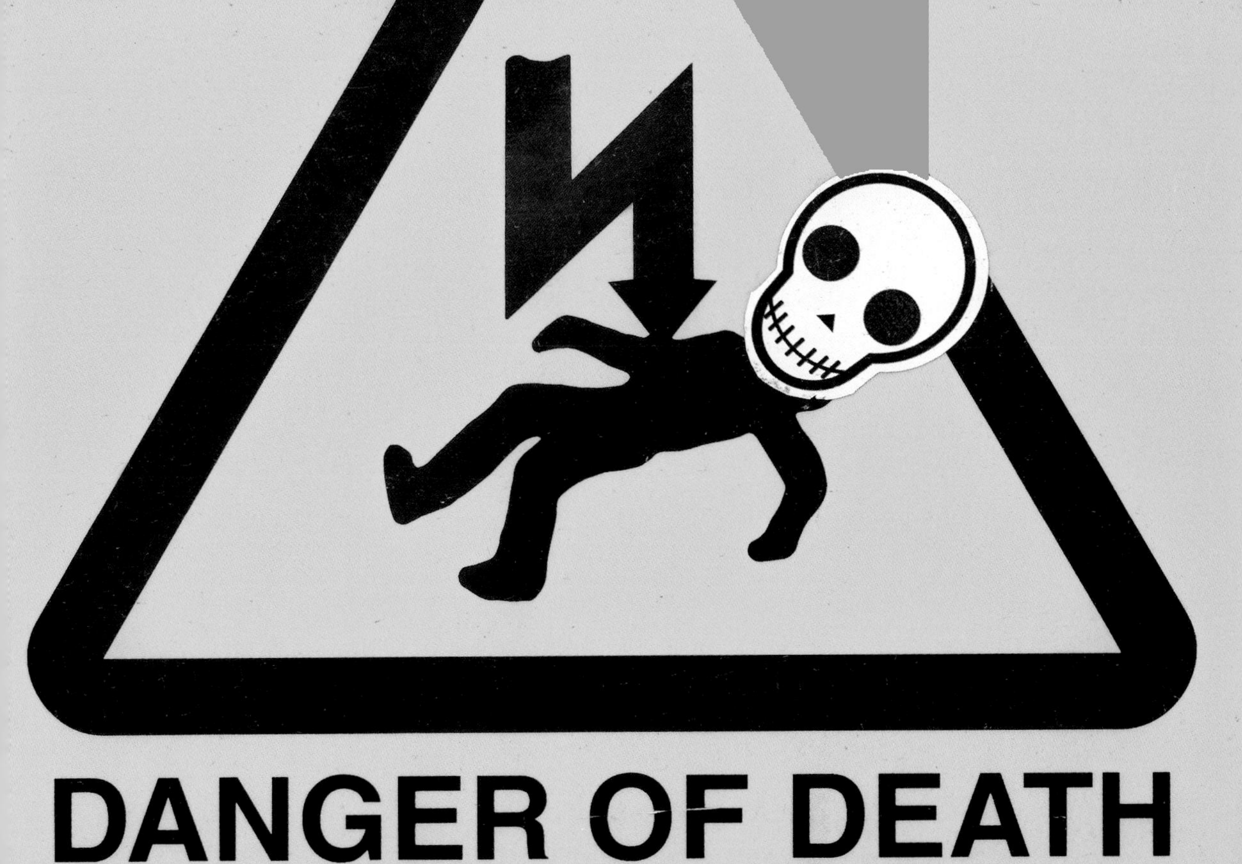
DANGER OF DEATH

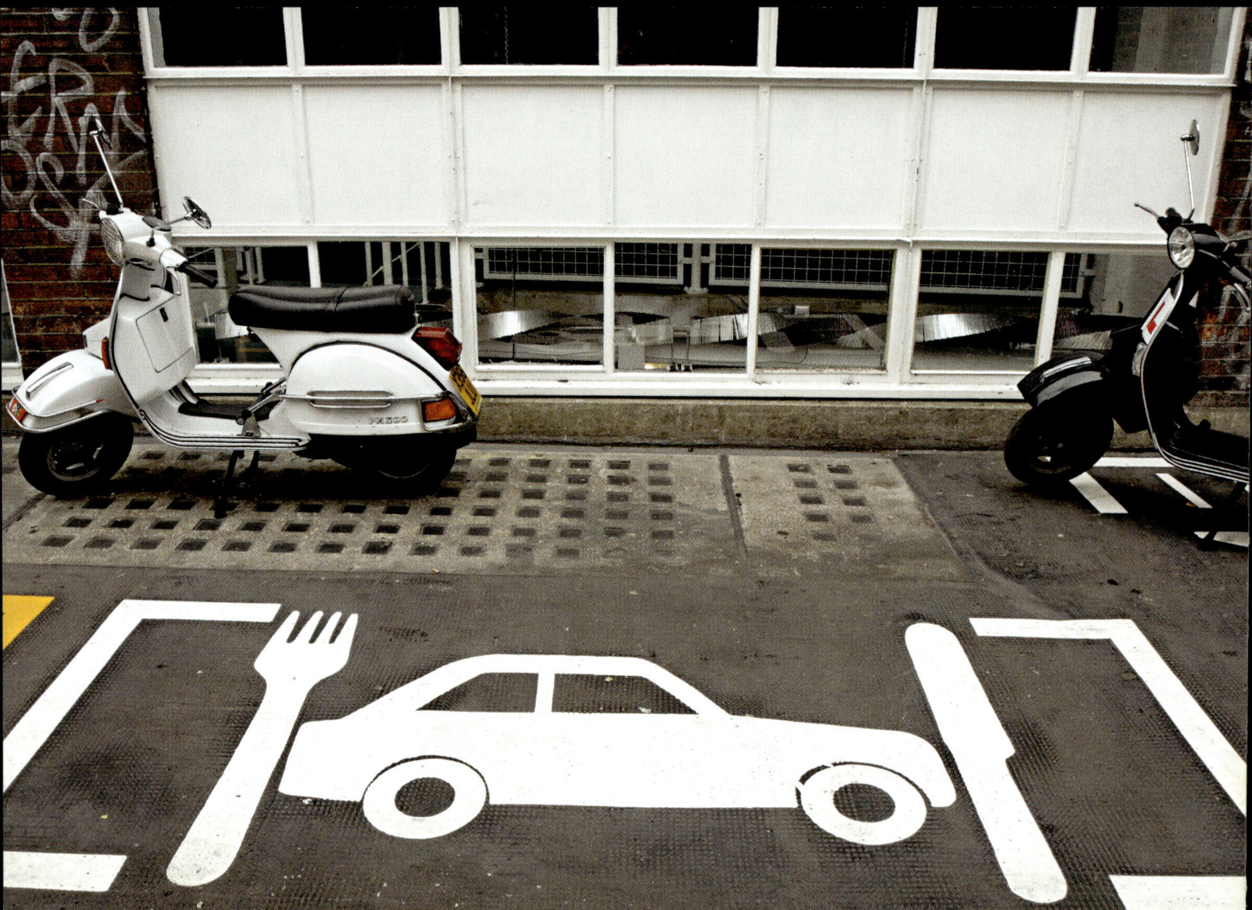

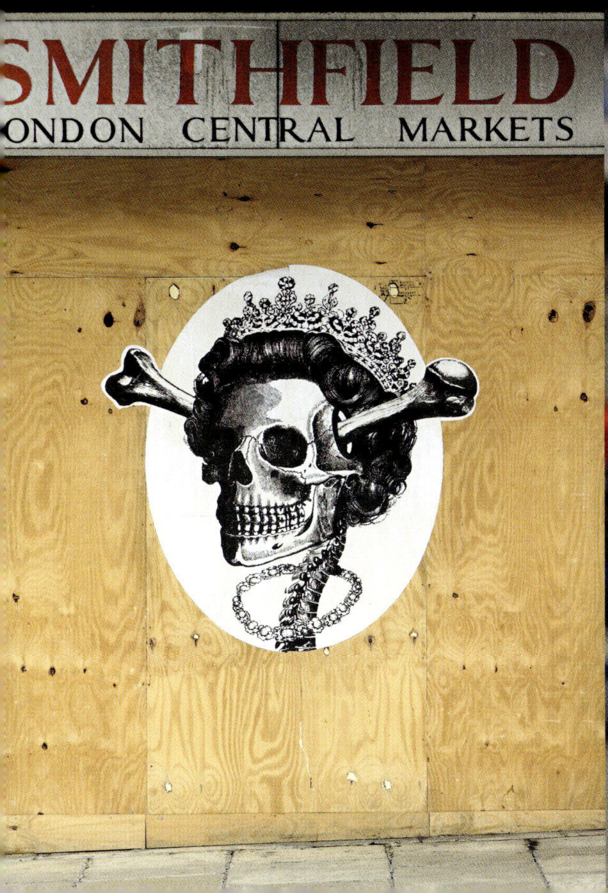

SMITHFIELD
ONDON CENTRAL MARKETS

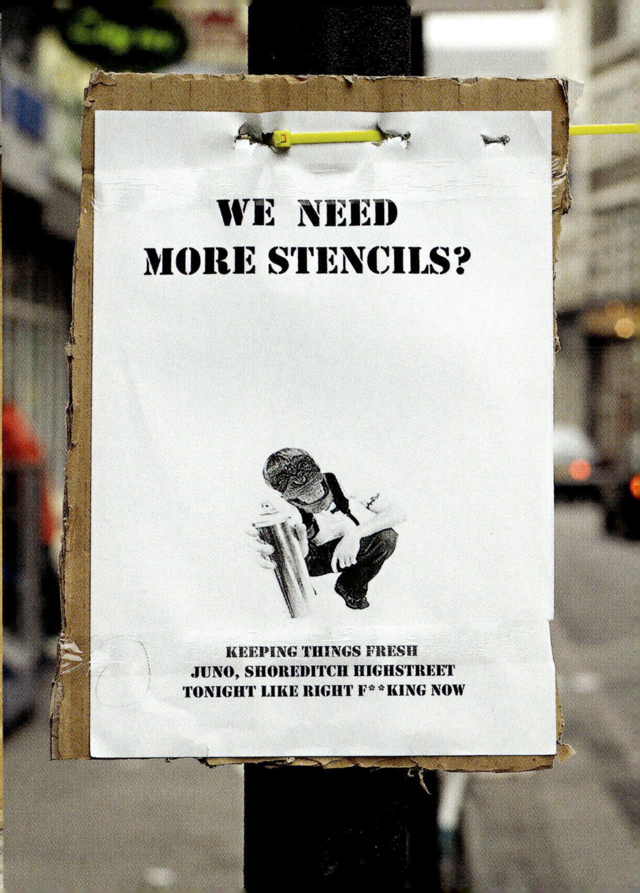

WE NEED
MORE STENCILS?

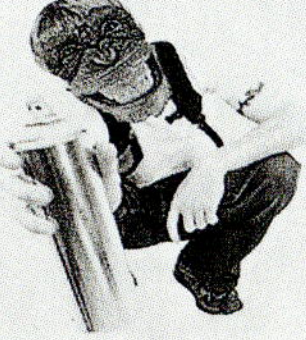

KEEPING THINGS FRESH
JUNO, SHOREDITCH HIGHSTREET
TONIGHT LIKE RIGHT F**KING NOW

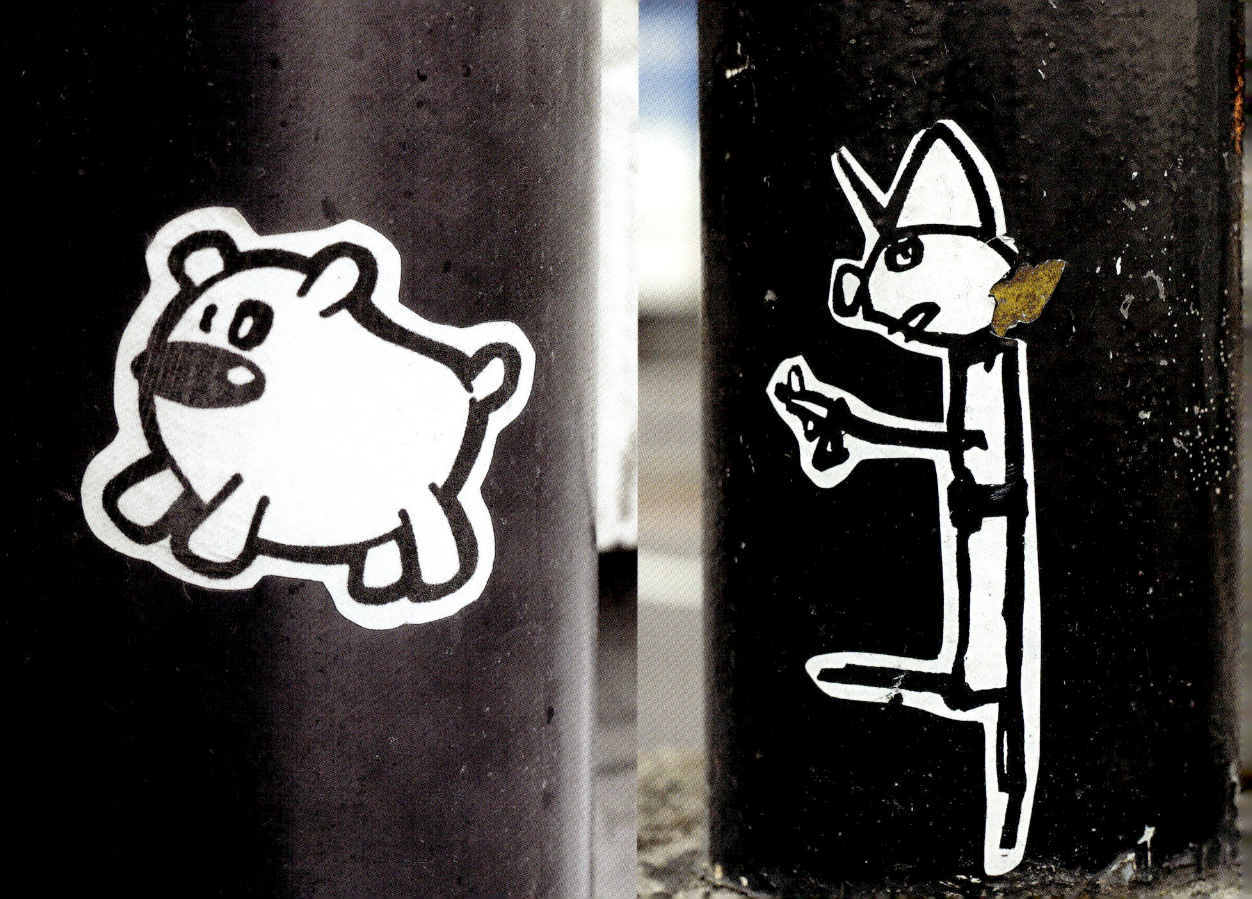

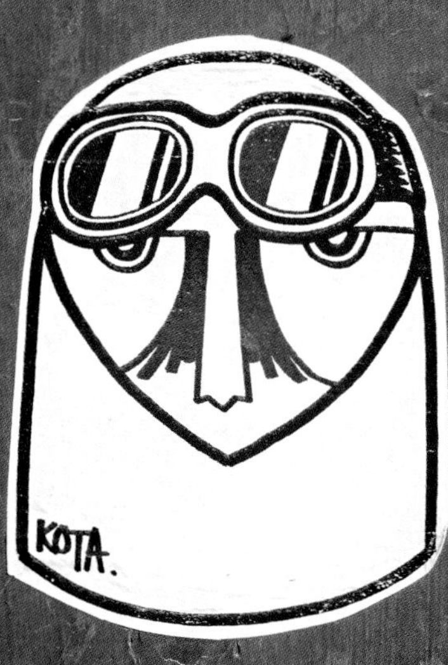
KOTA.
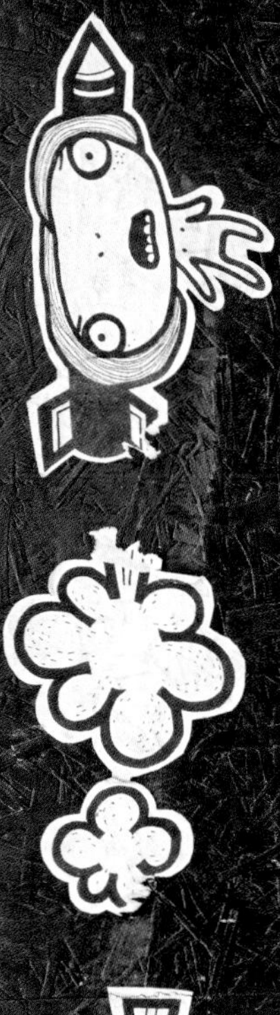
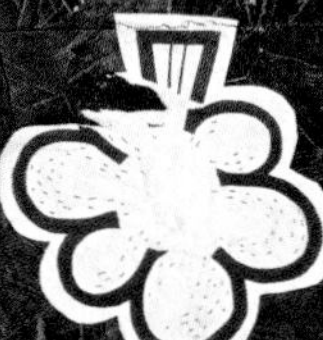

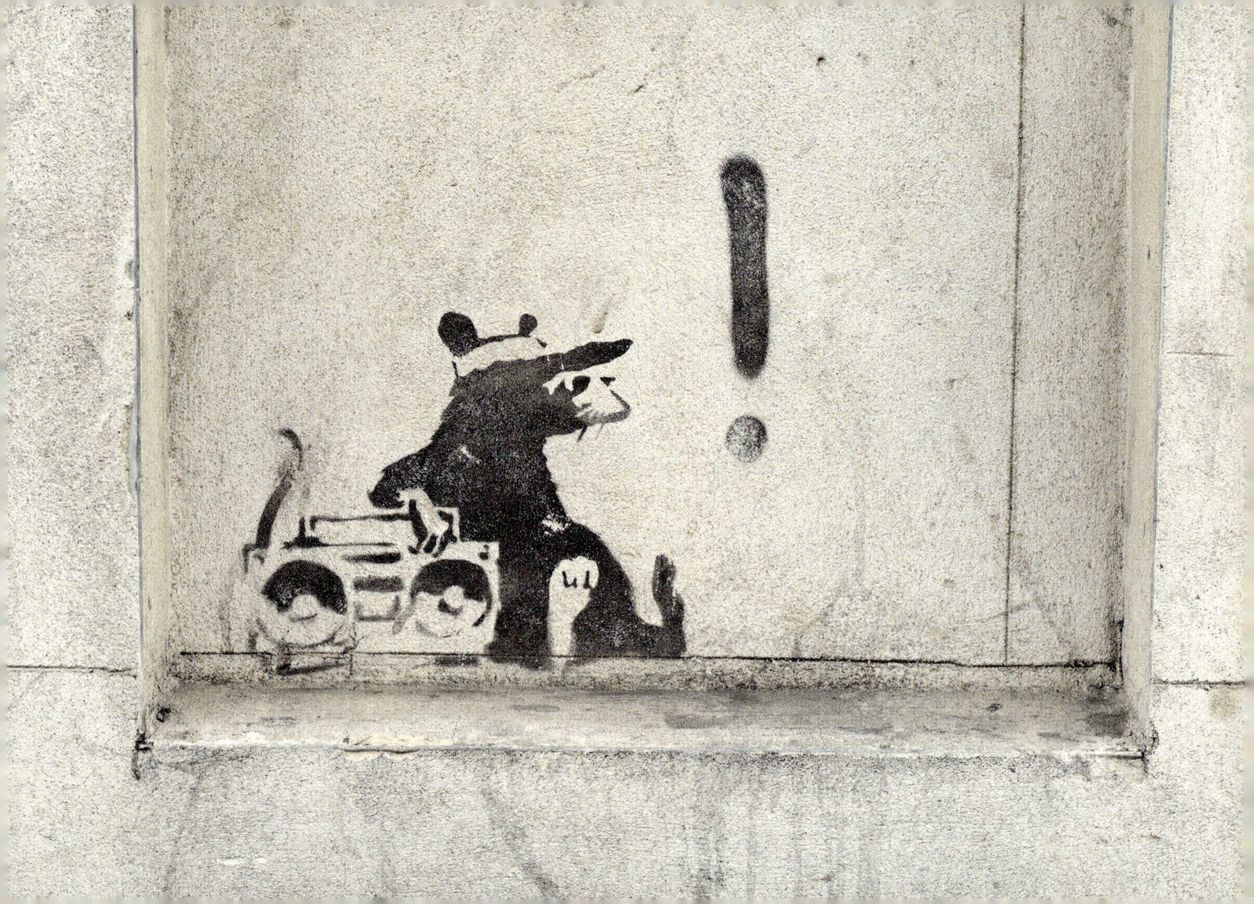

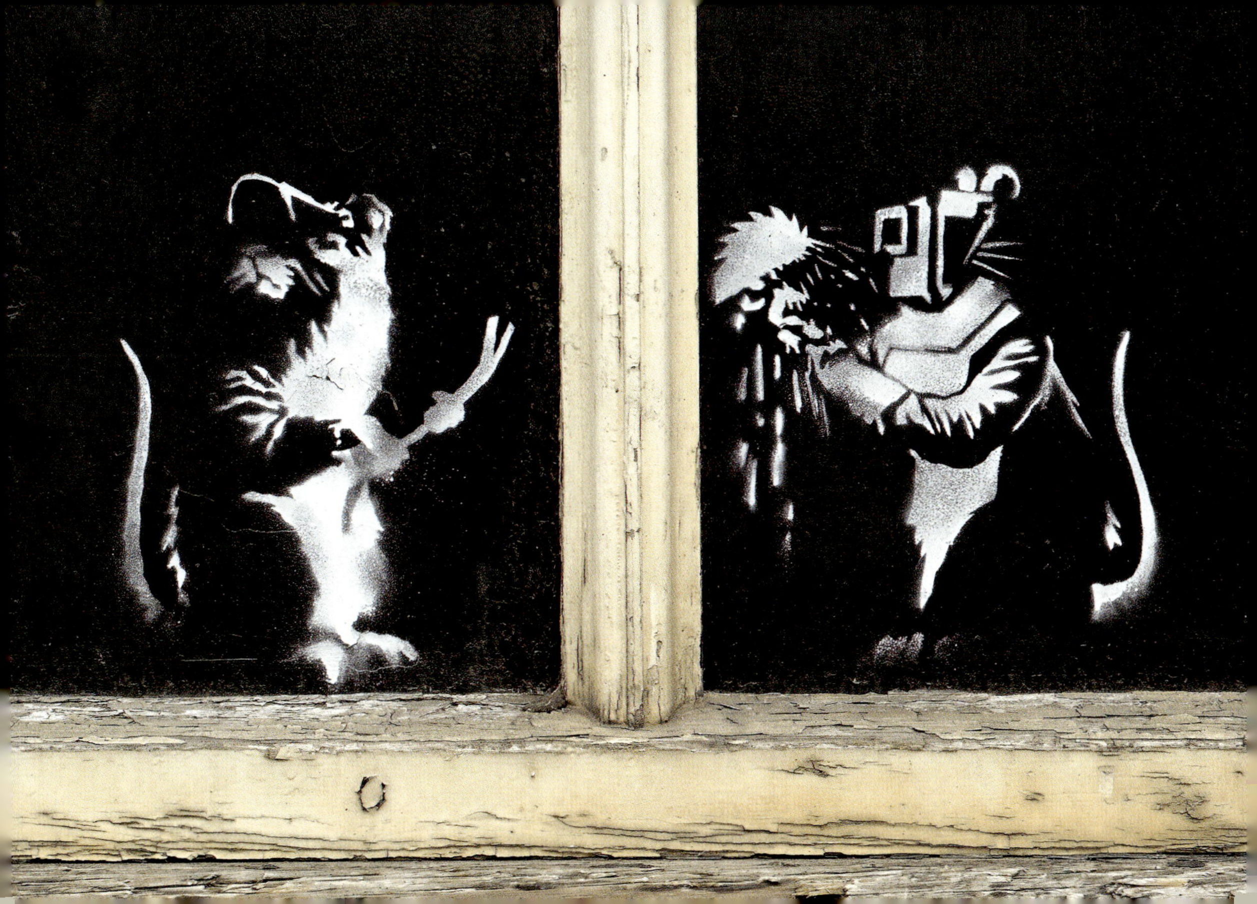

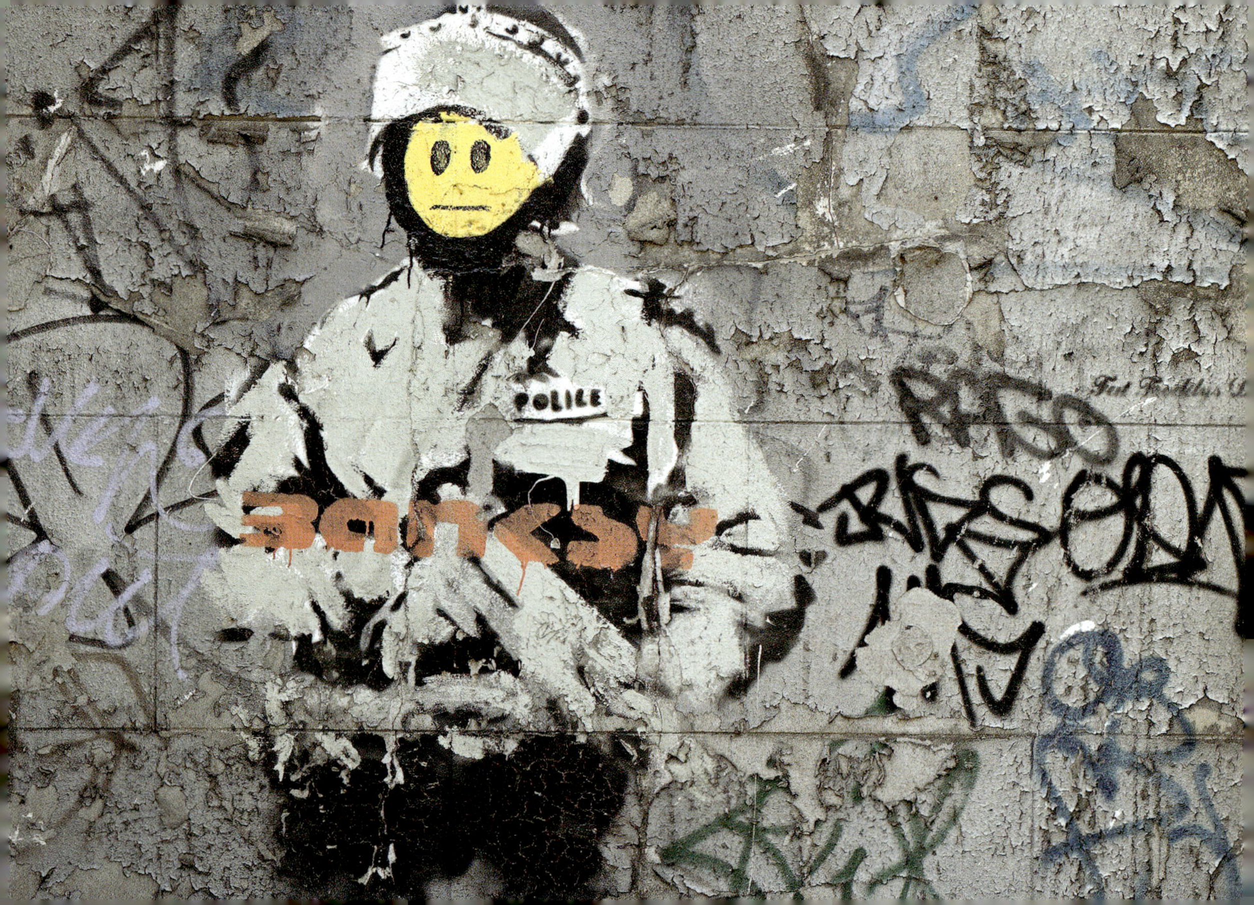
POLICE

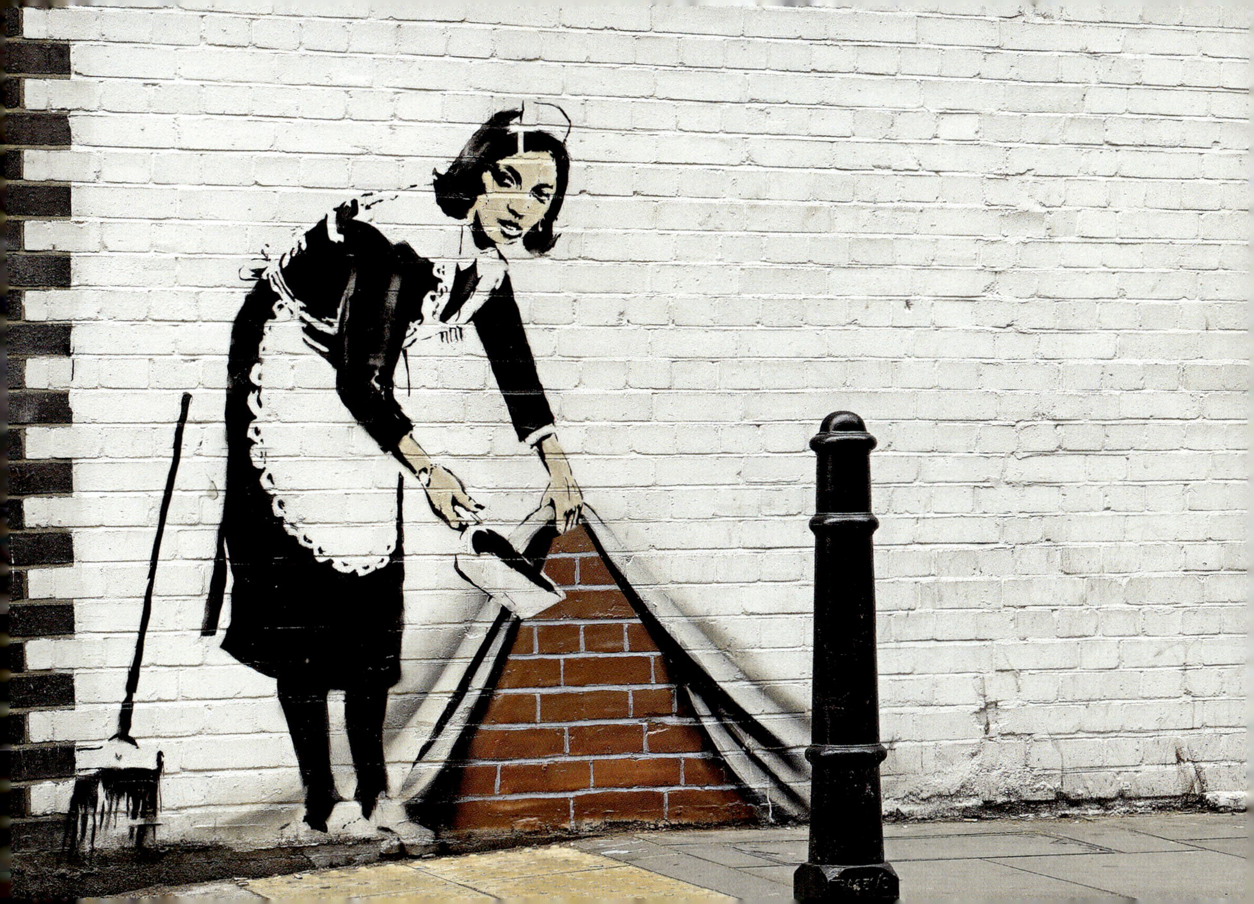

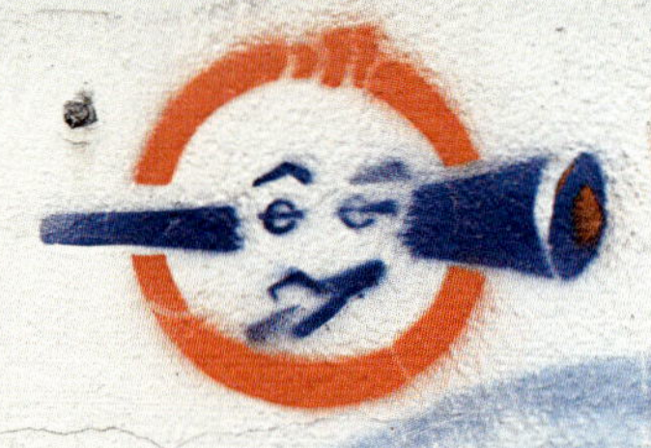
LONDON
TRANSPORT

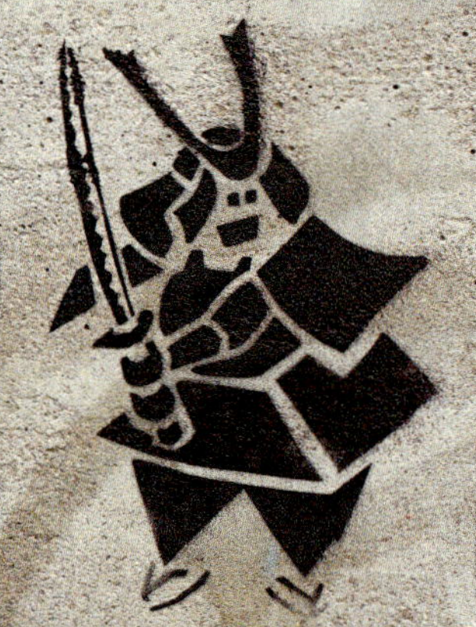

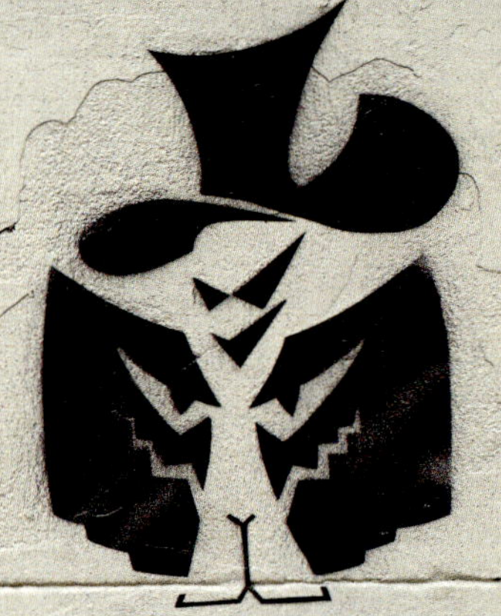

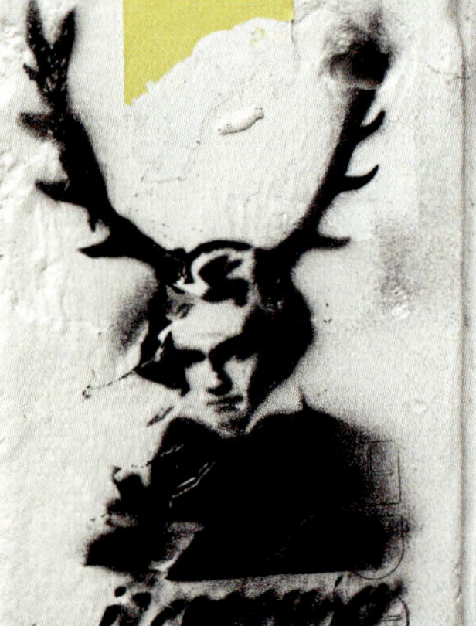

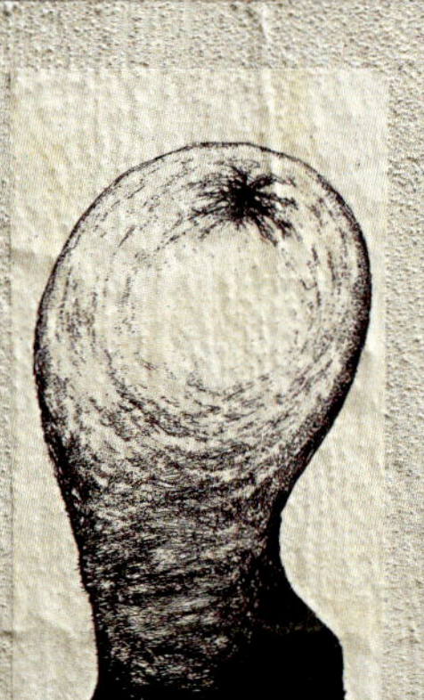

WARNING
CGTB
IN OPERATI

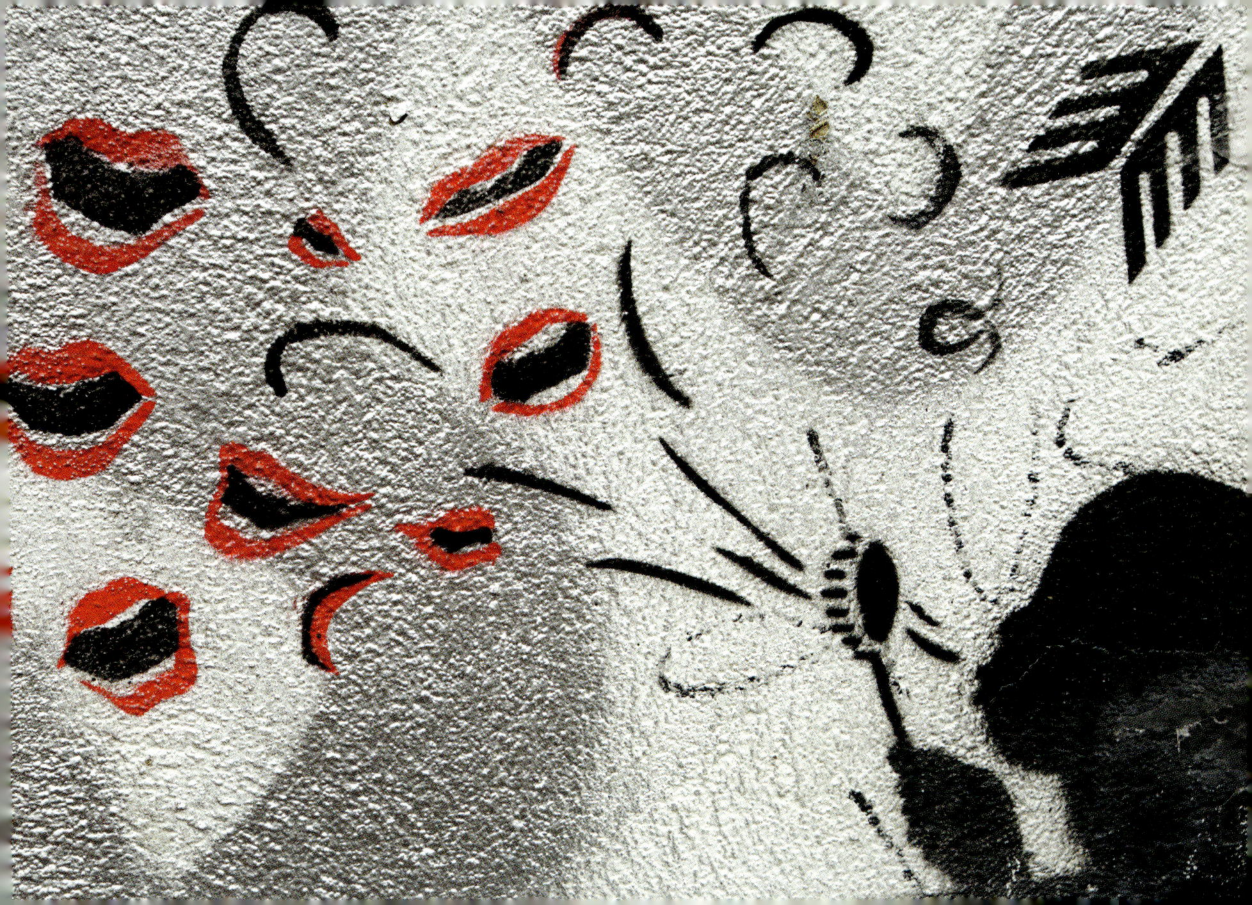

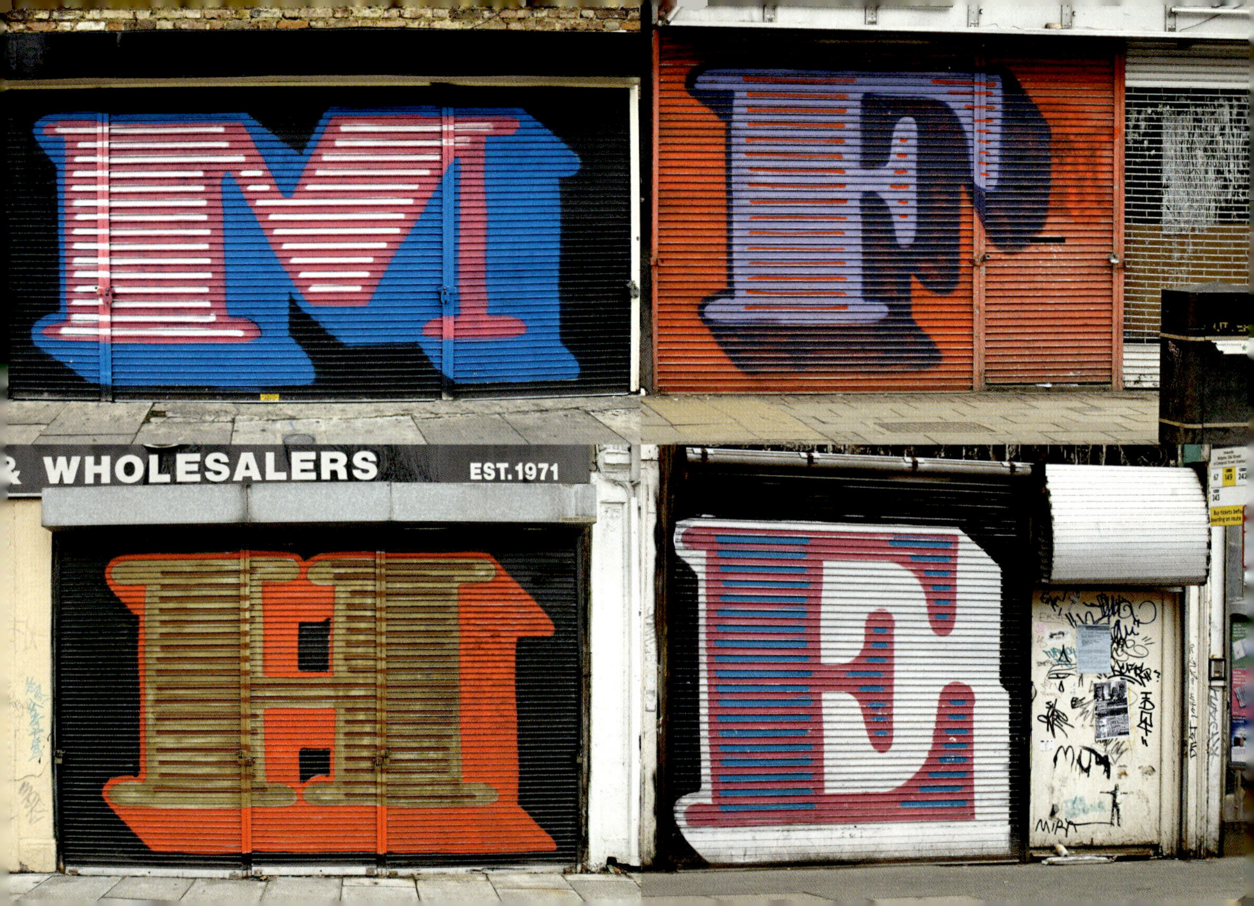
& WHOLESALERS
EST.1971

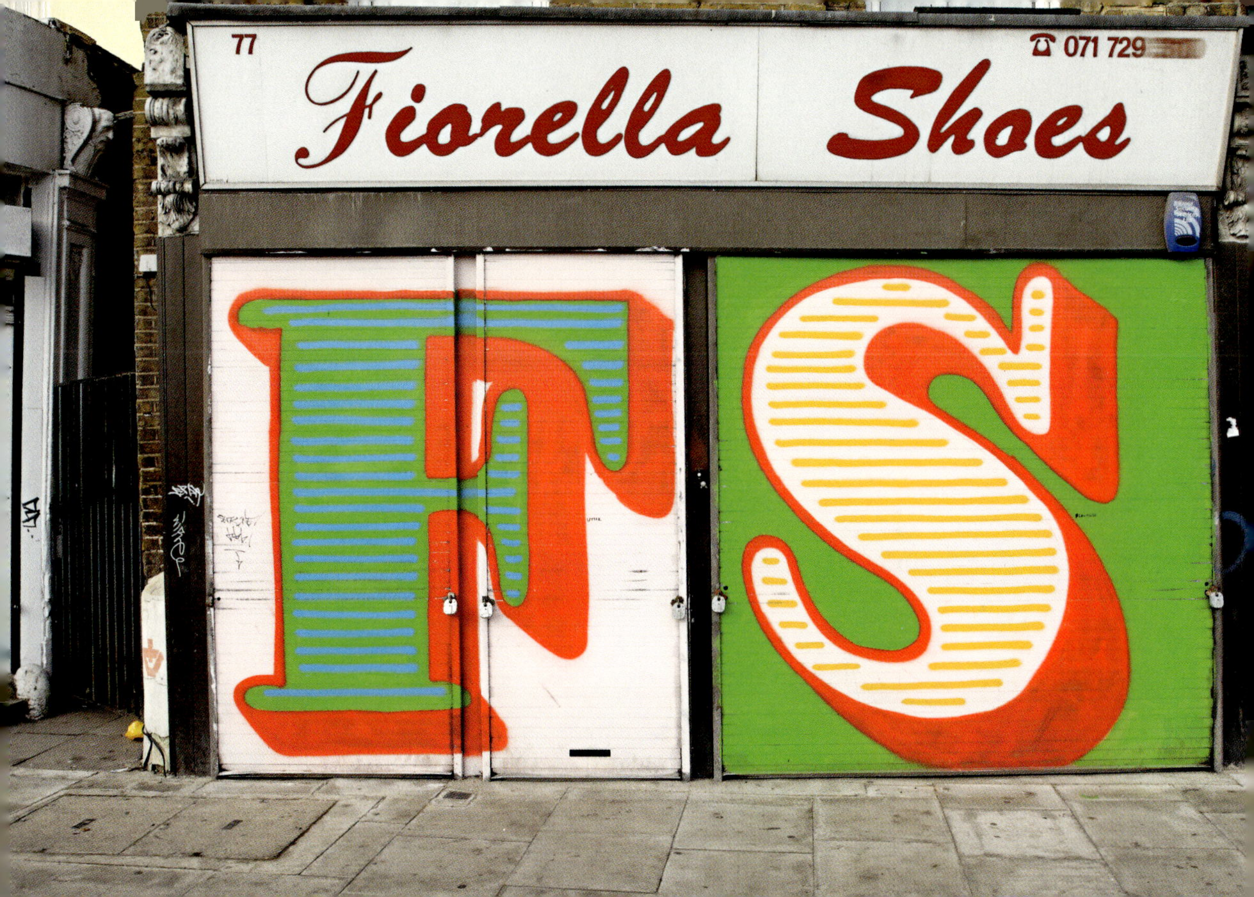
77
071 729
Fiorella Shoes
FS

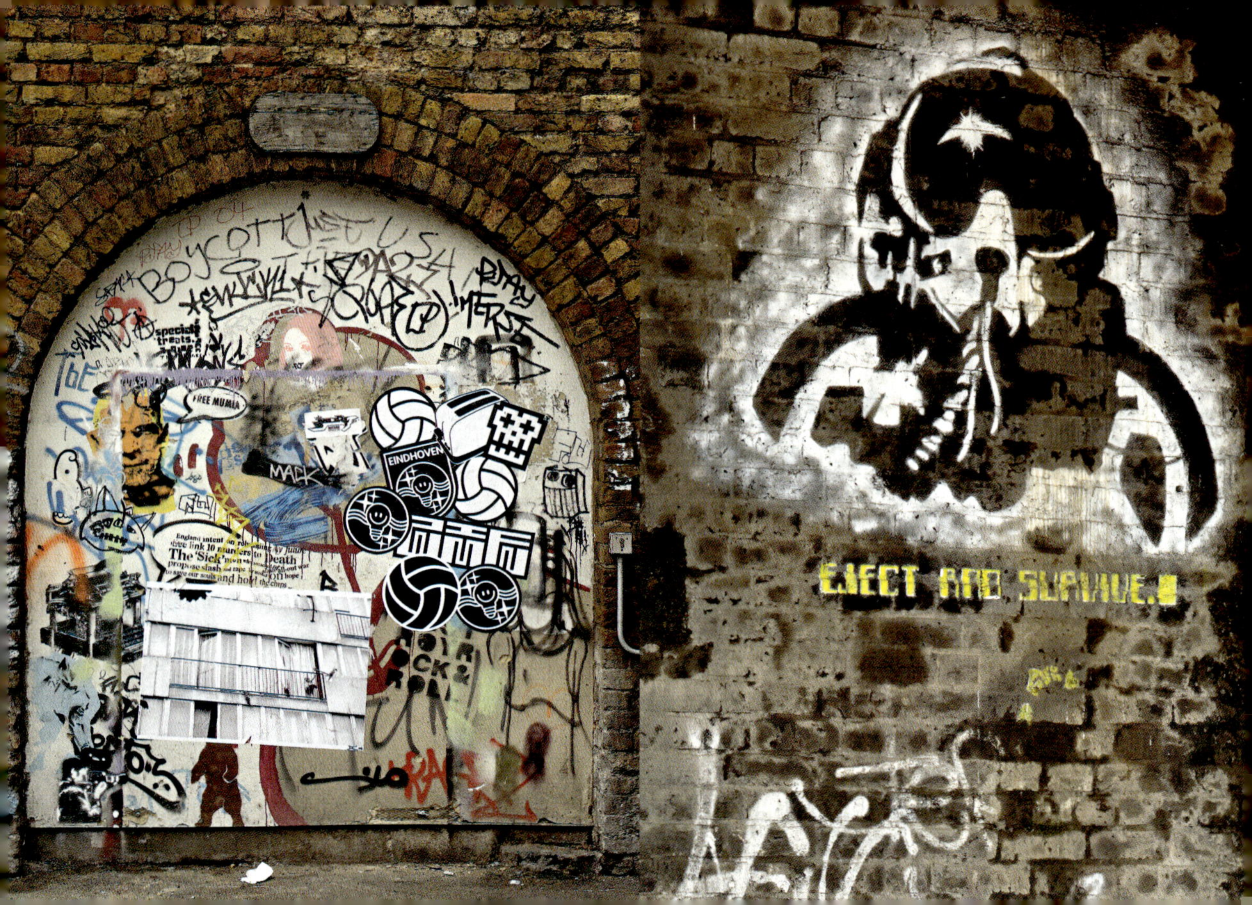

FREE MUMIA
EINDHOVEN
EJECT AND SURVIVE.

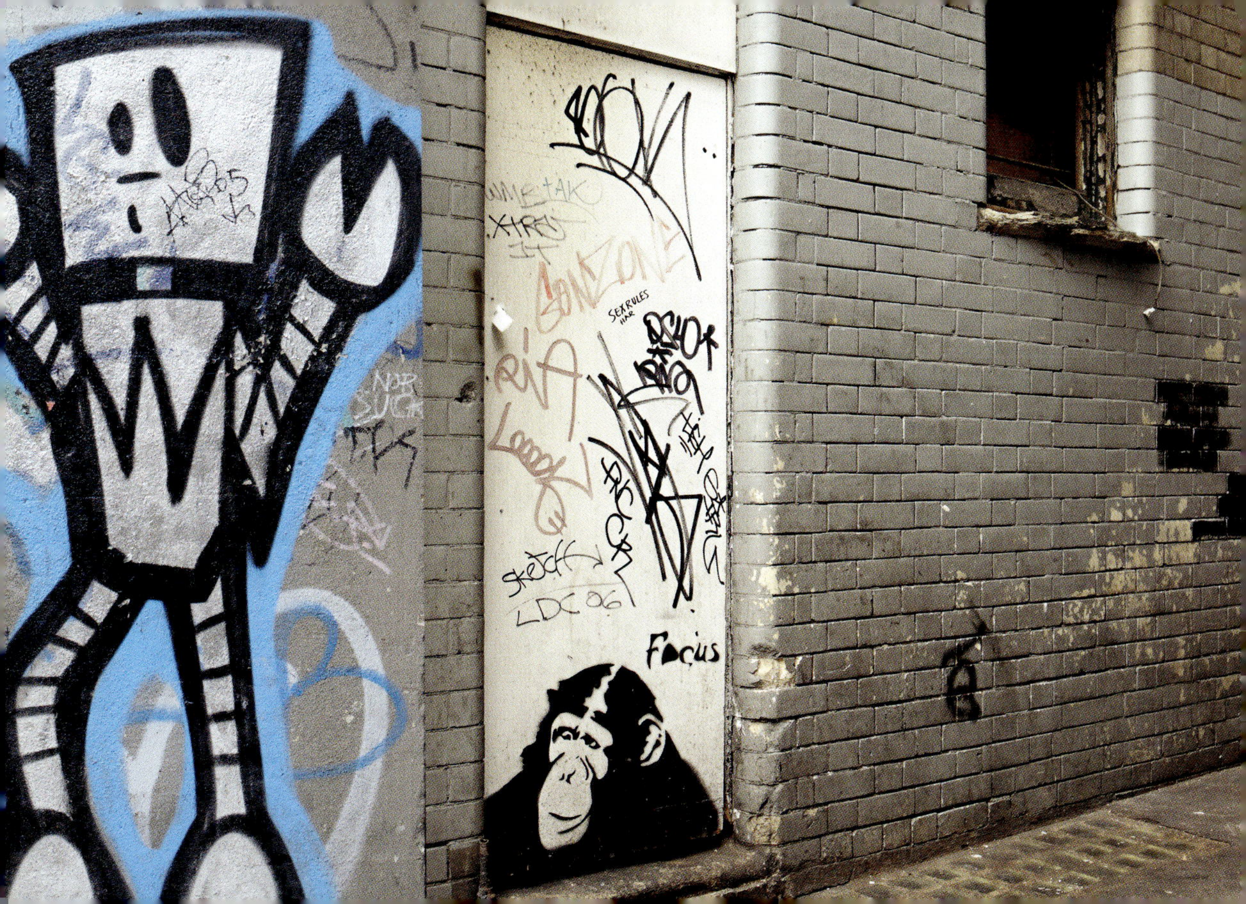
SEX RULES
LDC 06
Focus

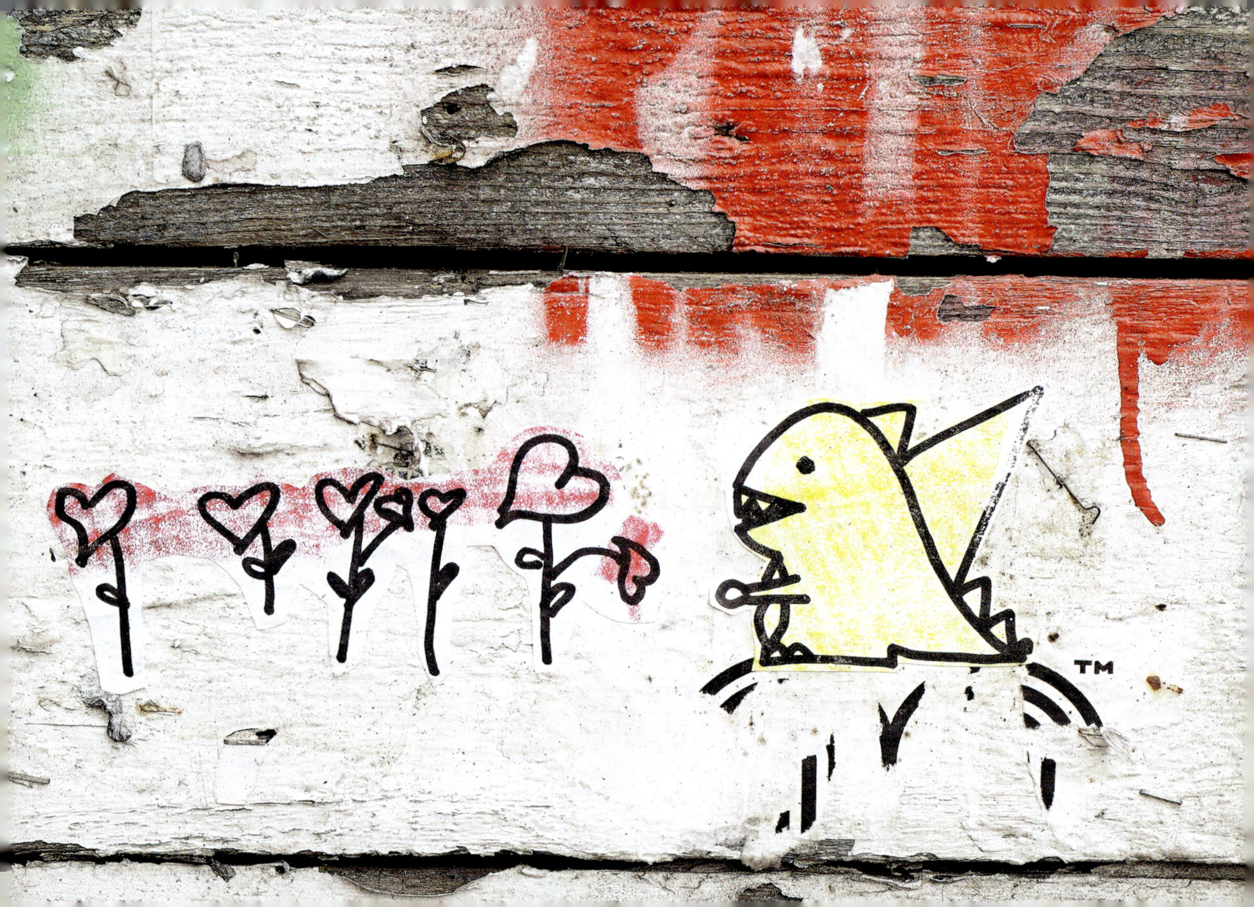
TM

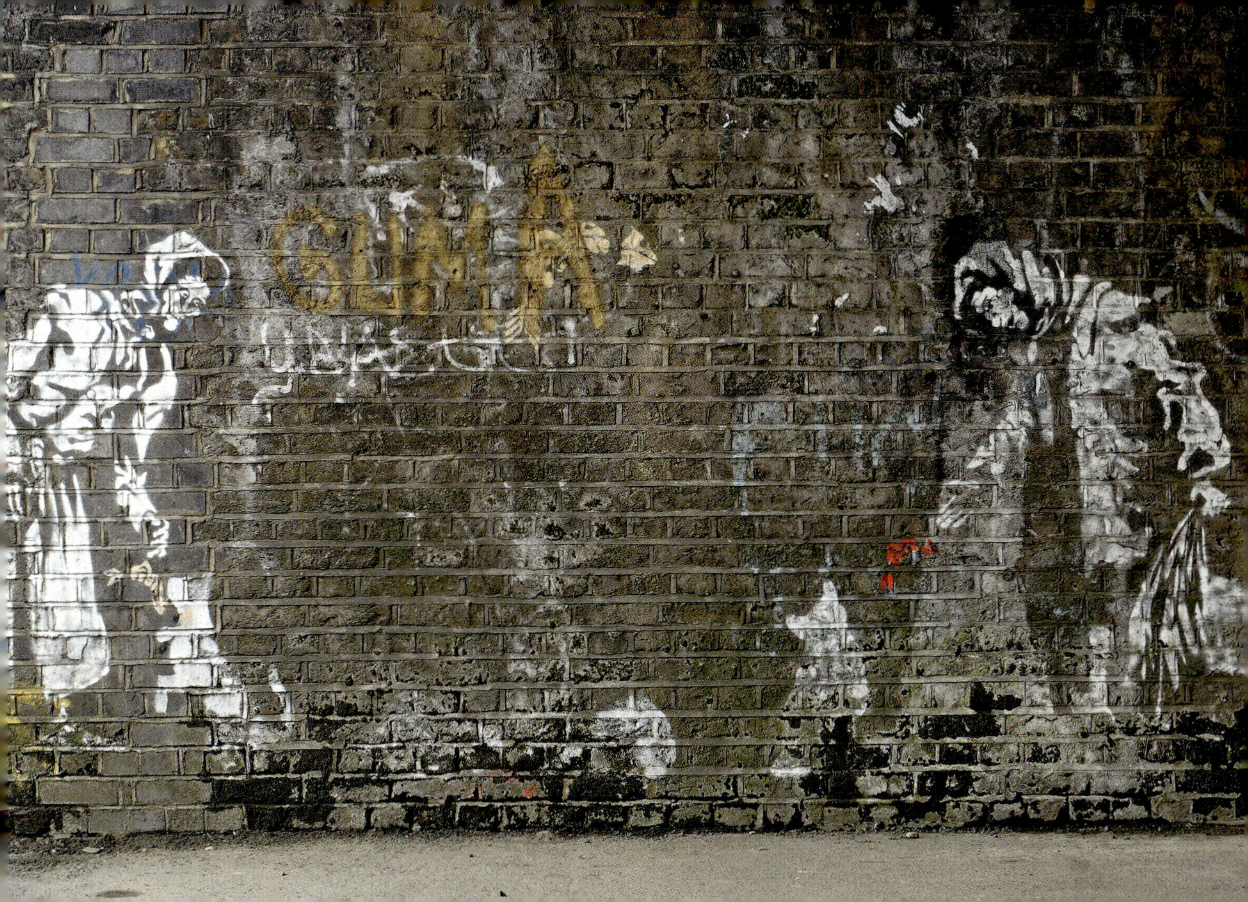

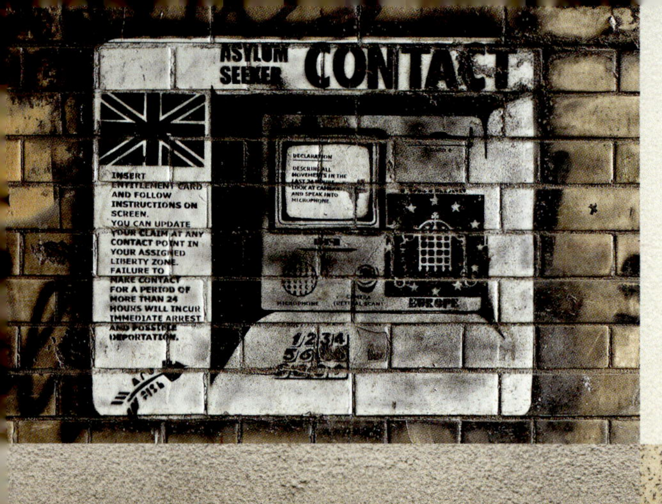
ASYLUM SEEKER
CONTACT
INSERT ENTITLEMENT CARD AND FOLLOW INSTRUCTIONS ON SCREEN. YOU CAN UPDATE YOUR CLAIM AT ANY CONTACT POINT IN YOUR ASSIGNED LIBERTY ZONE. FAILURE TO MAKE CONTACT FOR A PERIOD OF MORE THAN 24 HOURS WILL INCUR IMMEDIATE ARREST AND POSSIBLE DEPORTATION.
DECLARATION
DESCRIBE ALL MOVEMENTS IN THE
AND SPEAK INTO MICROPHONE
MICROPHONE
CAMERA (RETINAL SCAN)
EUROPE
1 2 3 4
5 6

THE JAWBREAKER ALL-CITY DELIVE
ALL WEATHER ★ ALL-SURFACES ★
FROM:
PETER DOHERTY
ALL CITY
FROM:
DO NOT REMOVE THIS LABEL

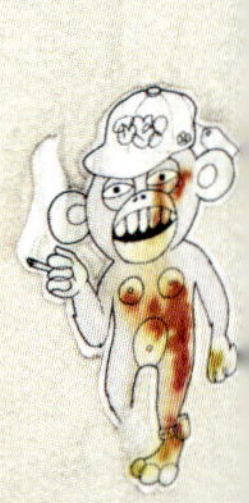

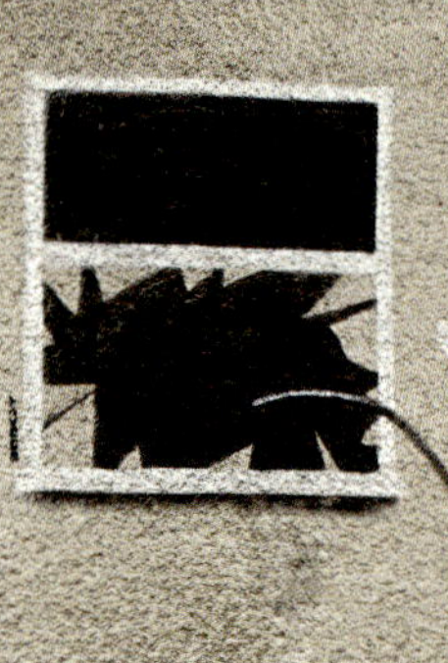

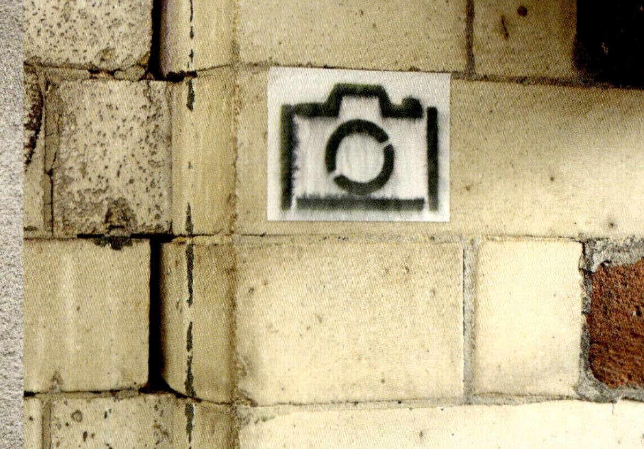

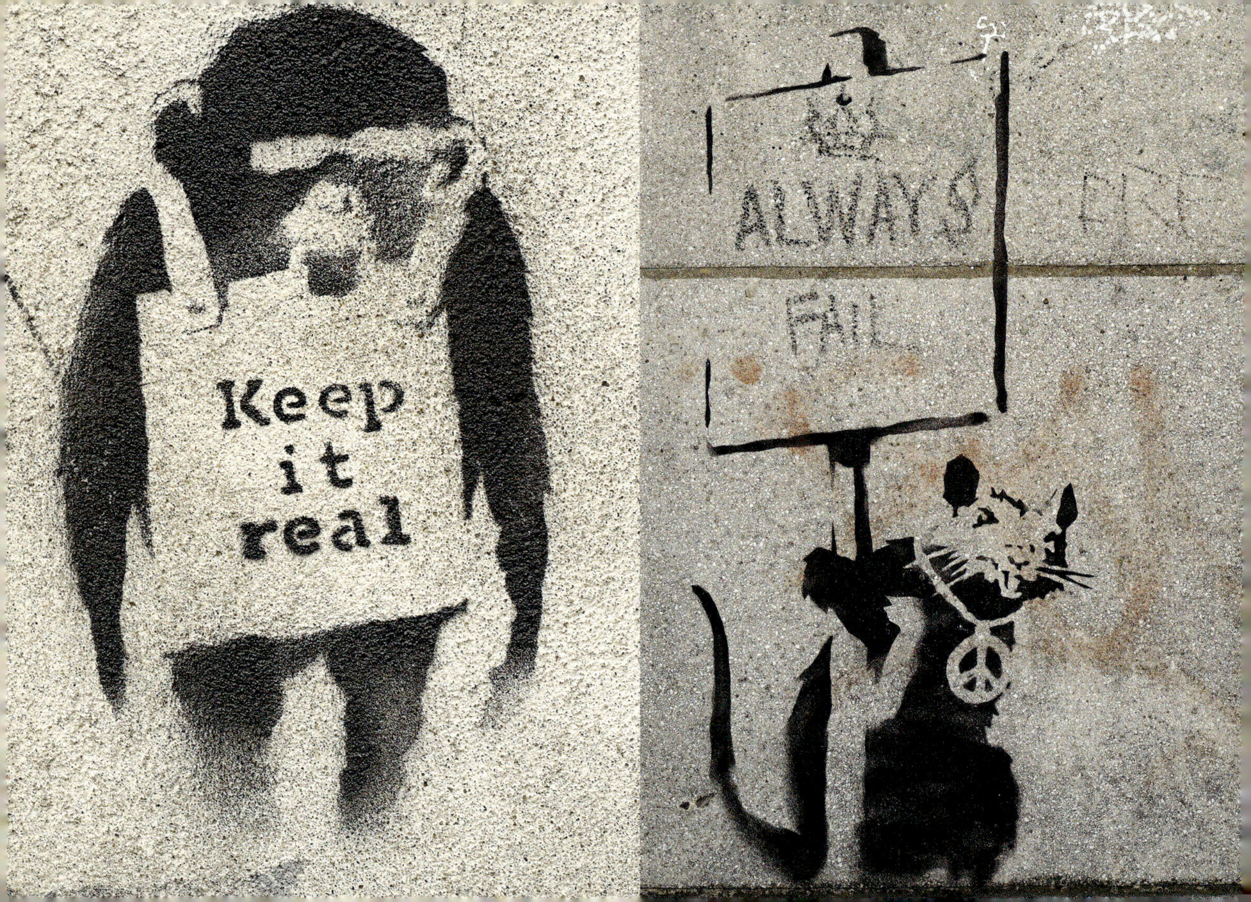
Keep it real
ALWAYS
FAIL

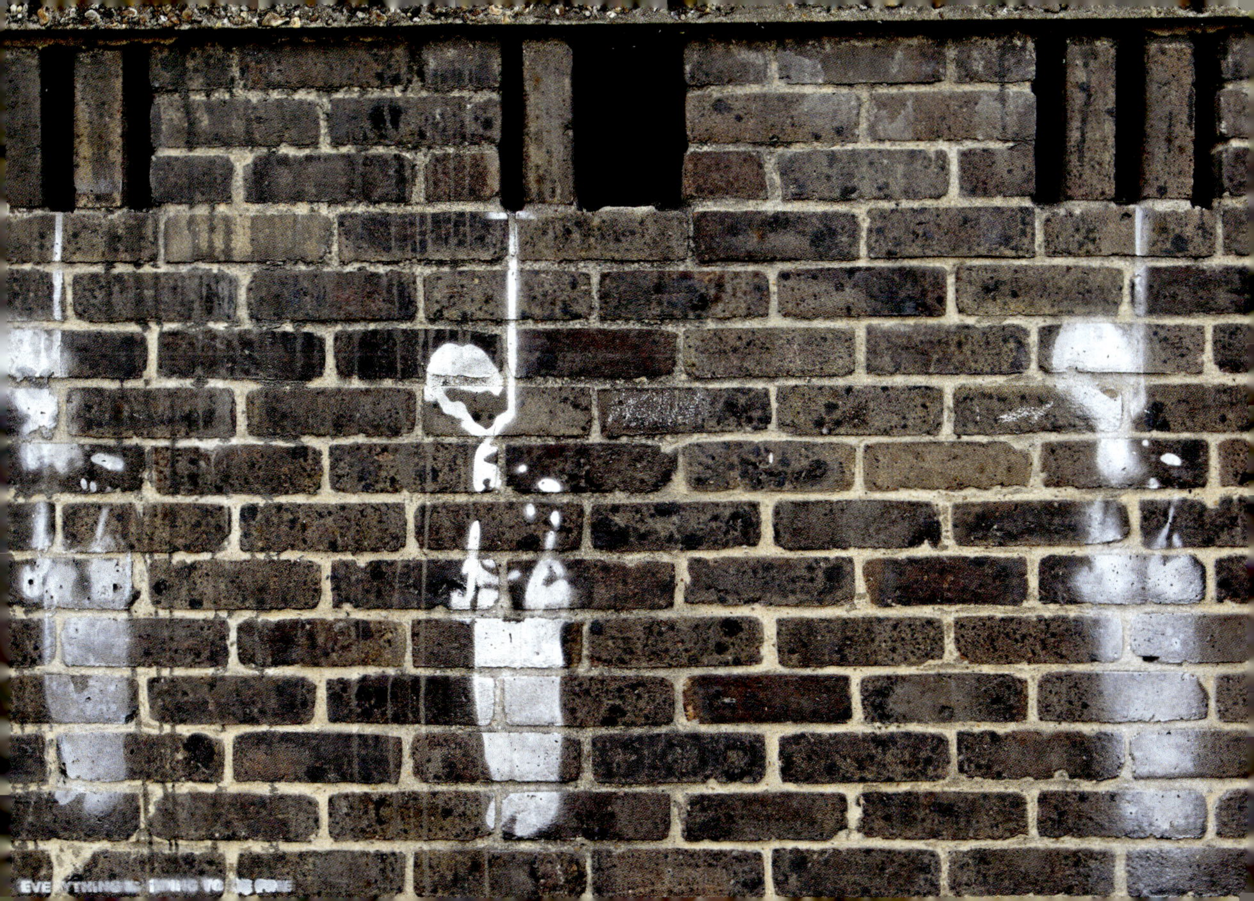

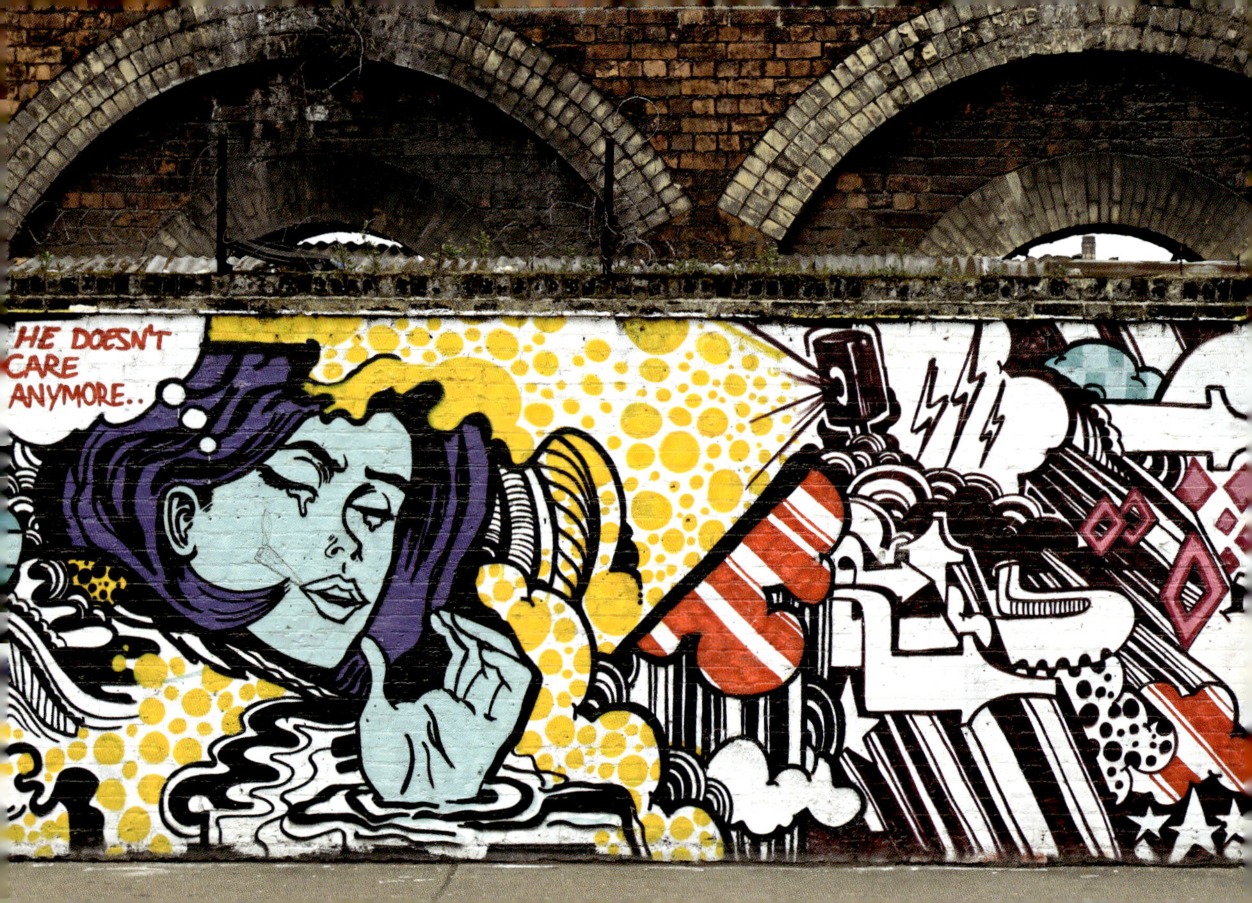
HE DOESN'T
CARE
ANYMORE..

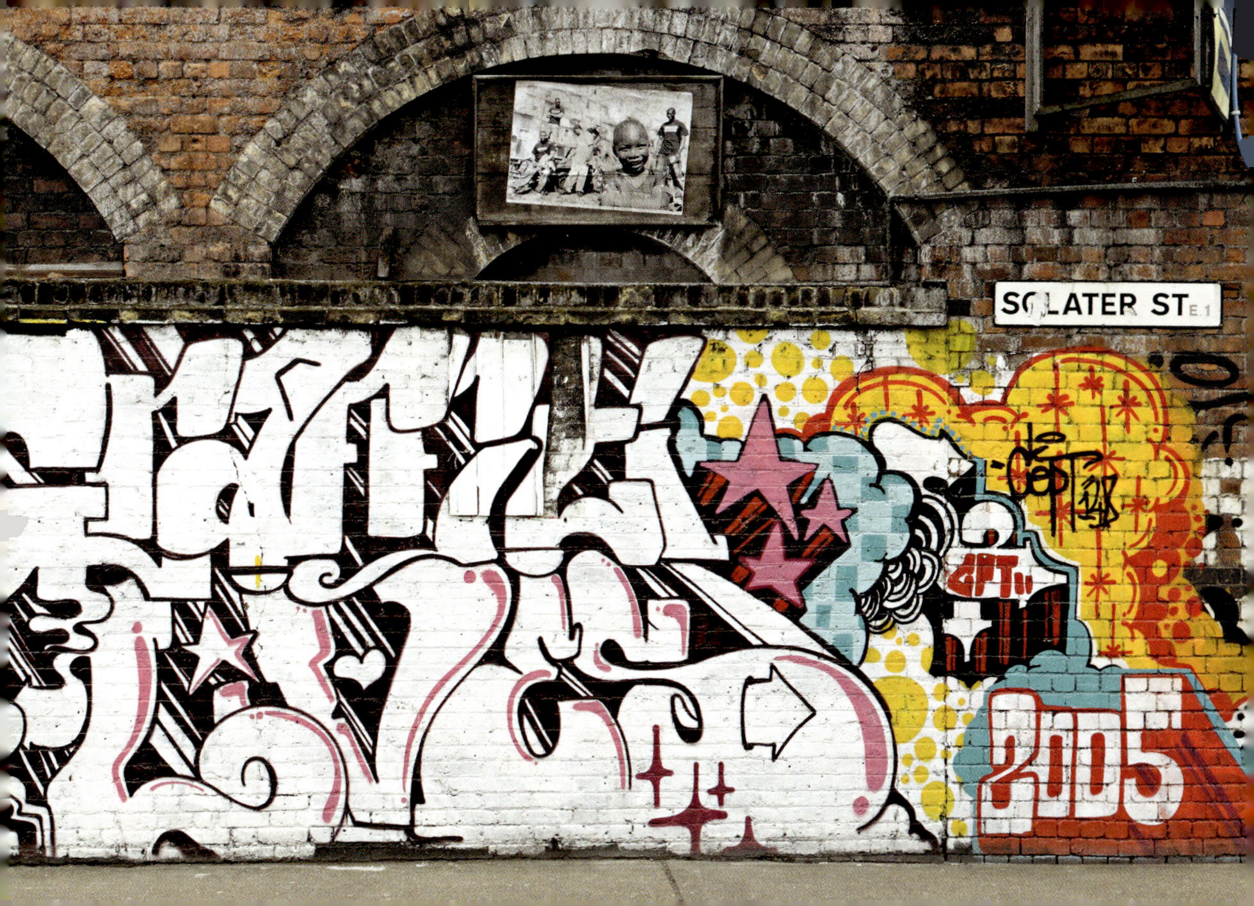
SCLATER ST E.1
2005

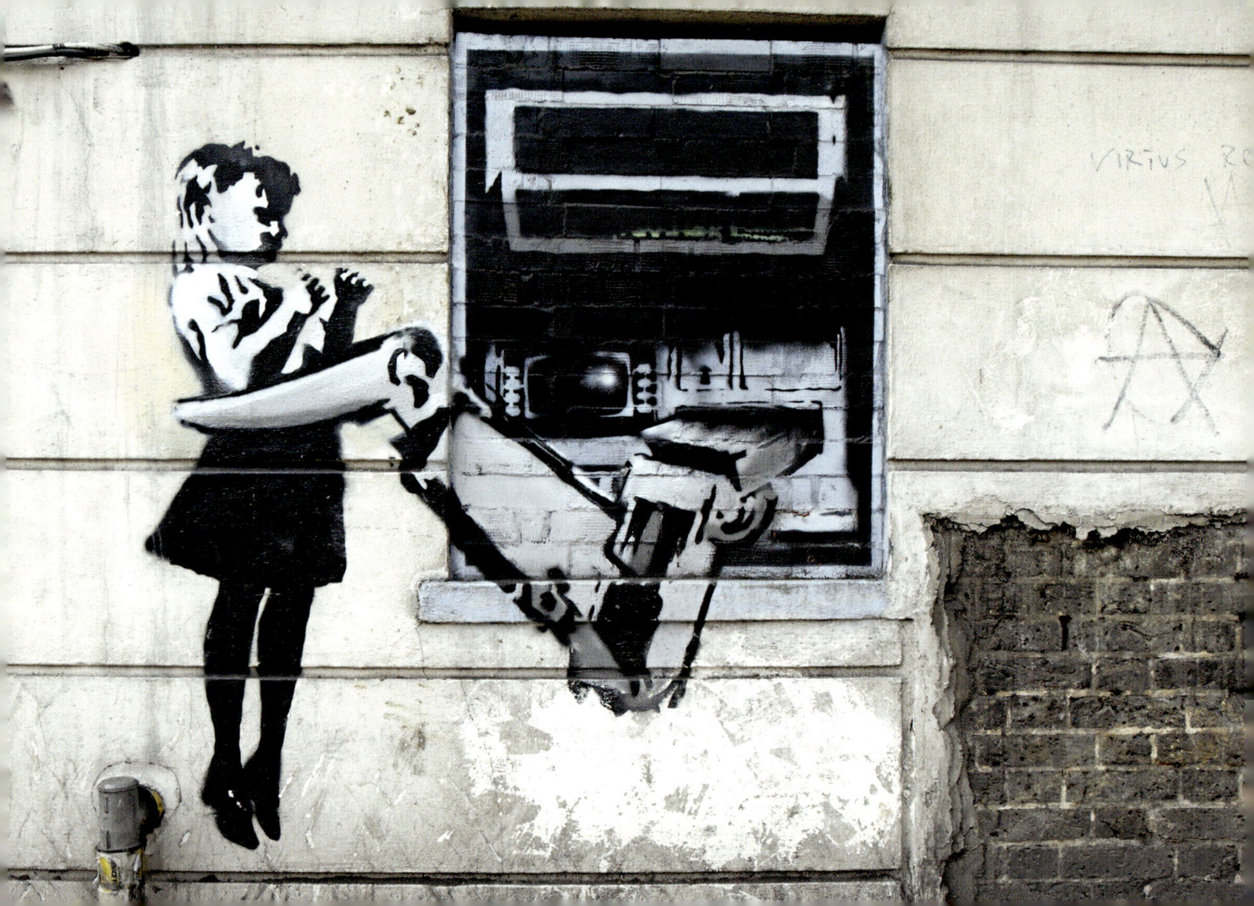
VIRTUS

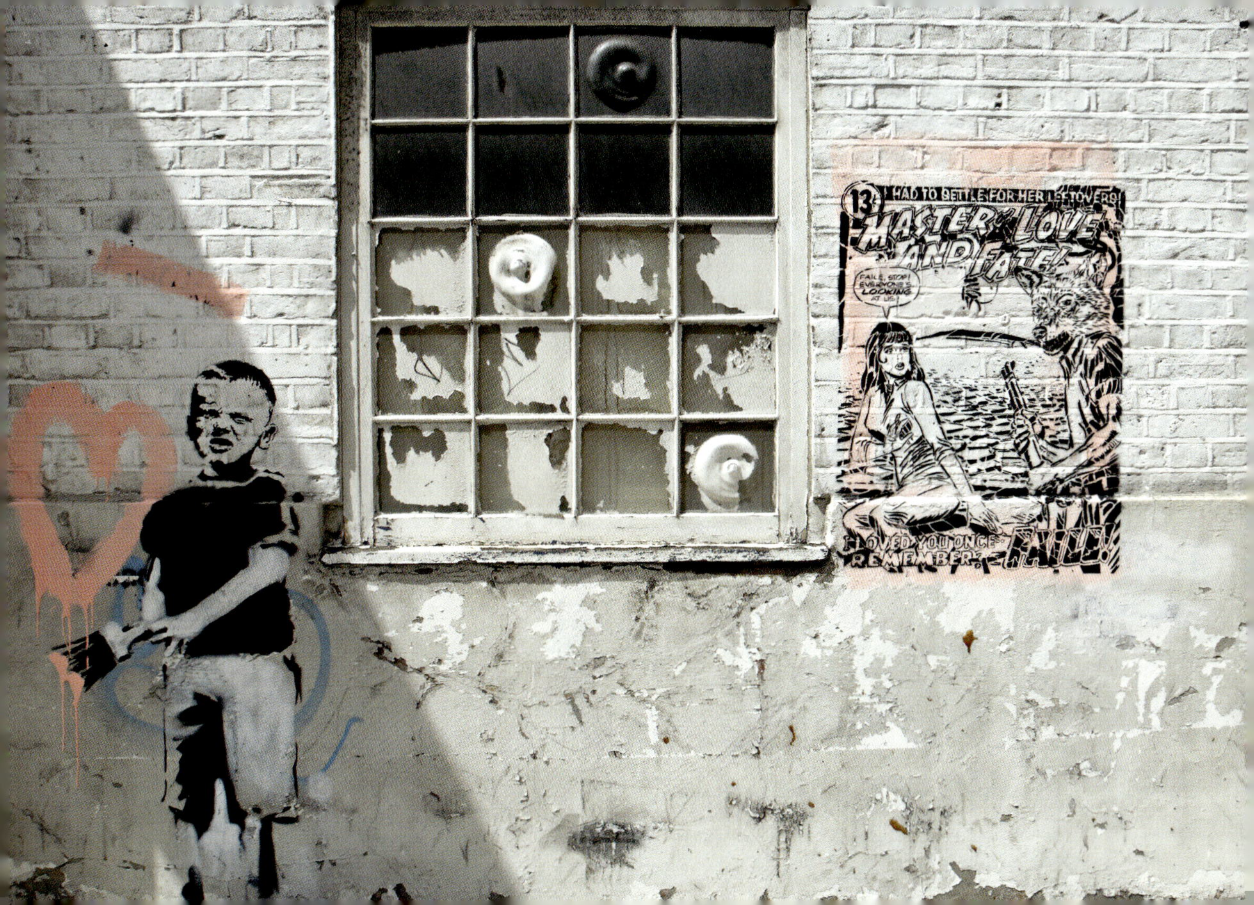
13¢
I HAD TO SETTLE FOR HER LEFTOVERS!
MASTER of LOVE AND FATE!
FAILE, STOP! EVERYONE'S LOOKING AT US!
I LOVED YOU ONCE- REMEMBER?
FAILE!

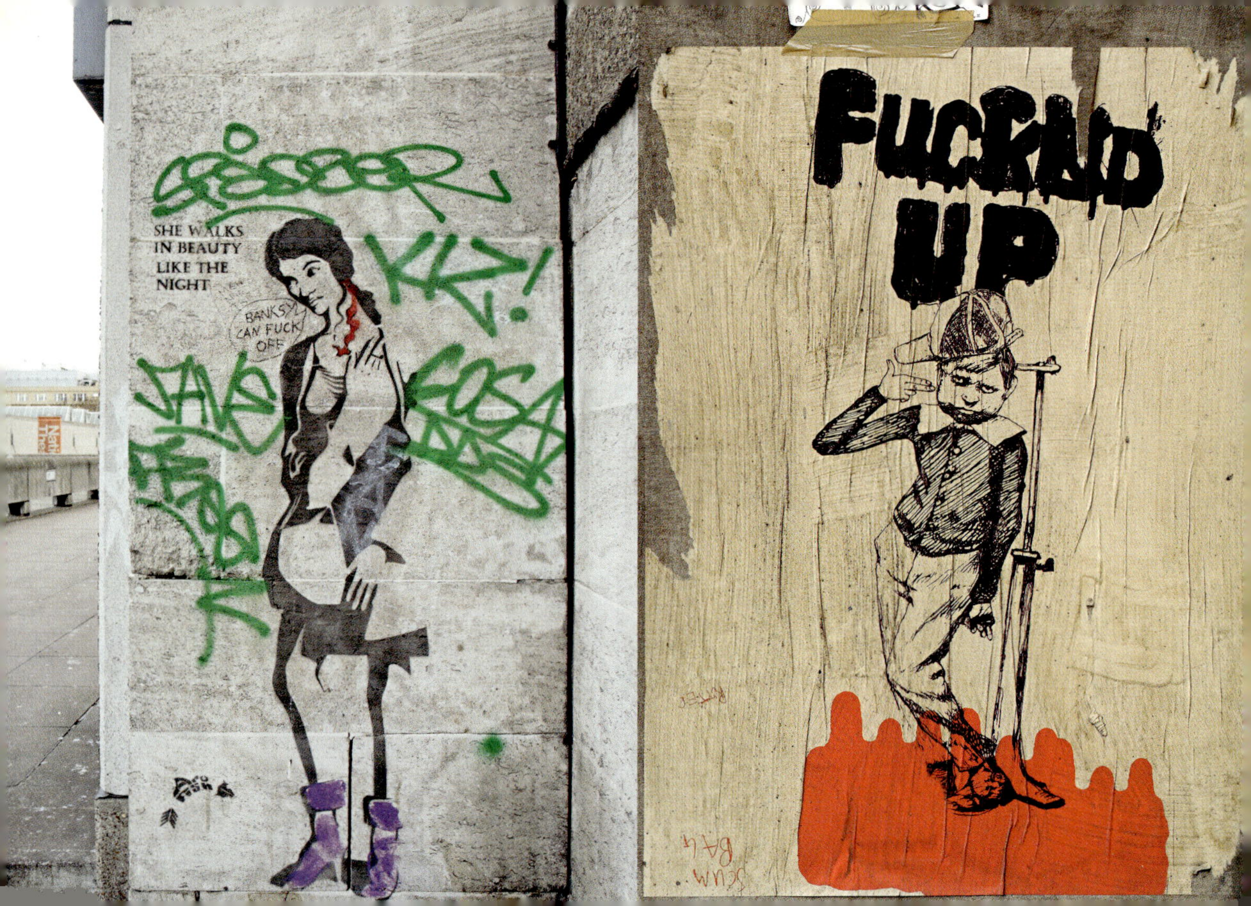
SHE WALKS
IN BEAUTY
LIKE THE
NIGHT
BANKSY
CAN FUCK
OFF

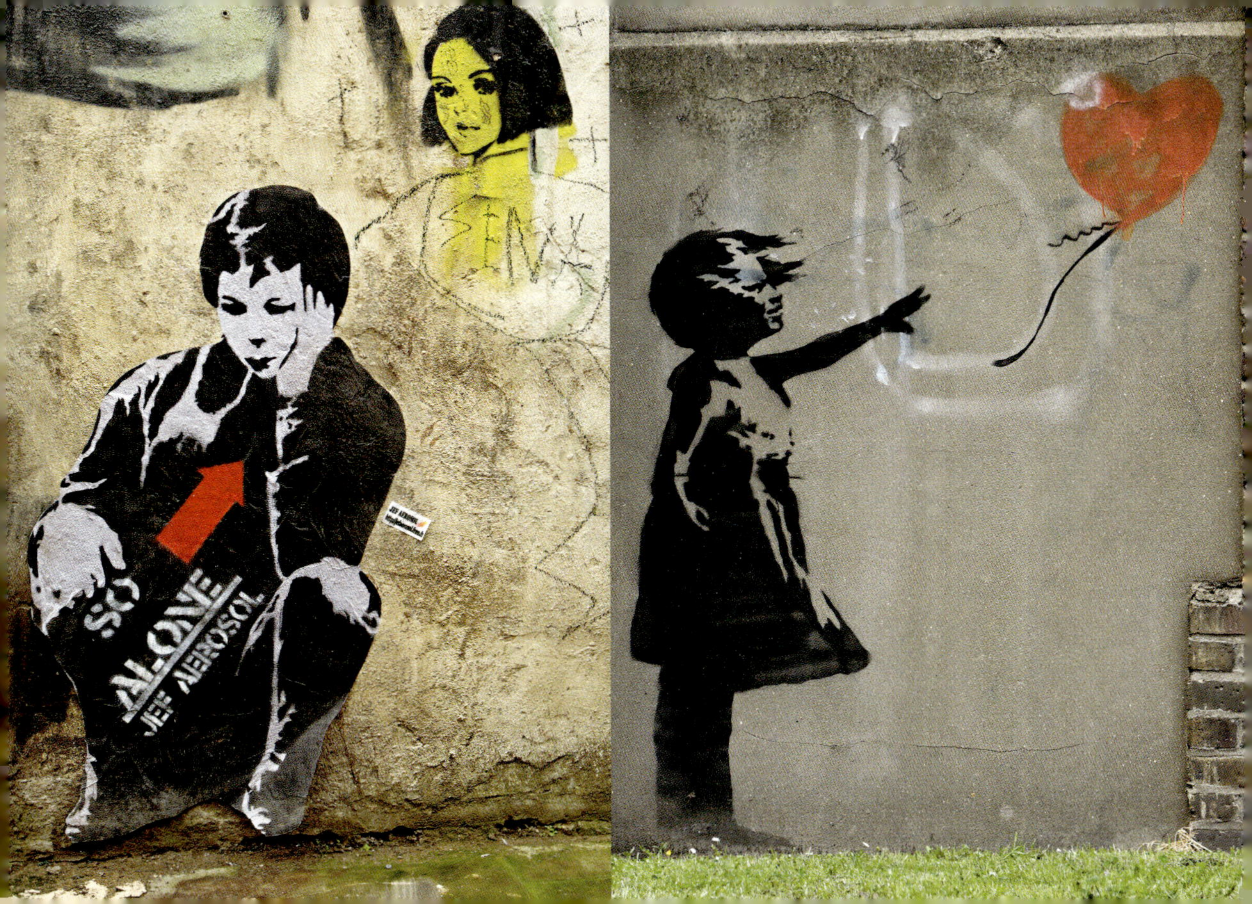
SO
ALONE
JEF AEROSOL

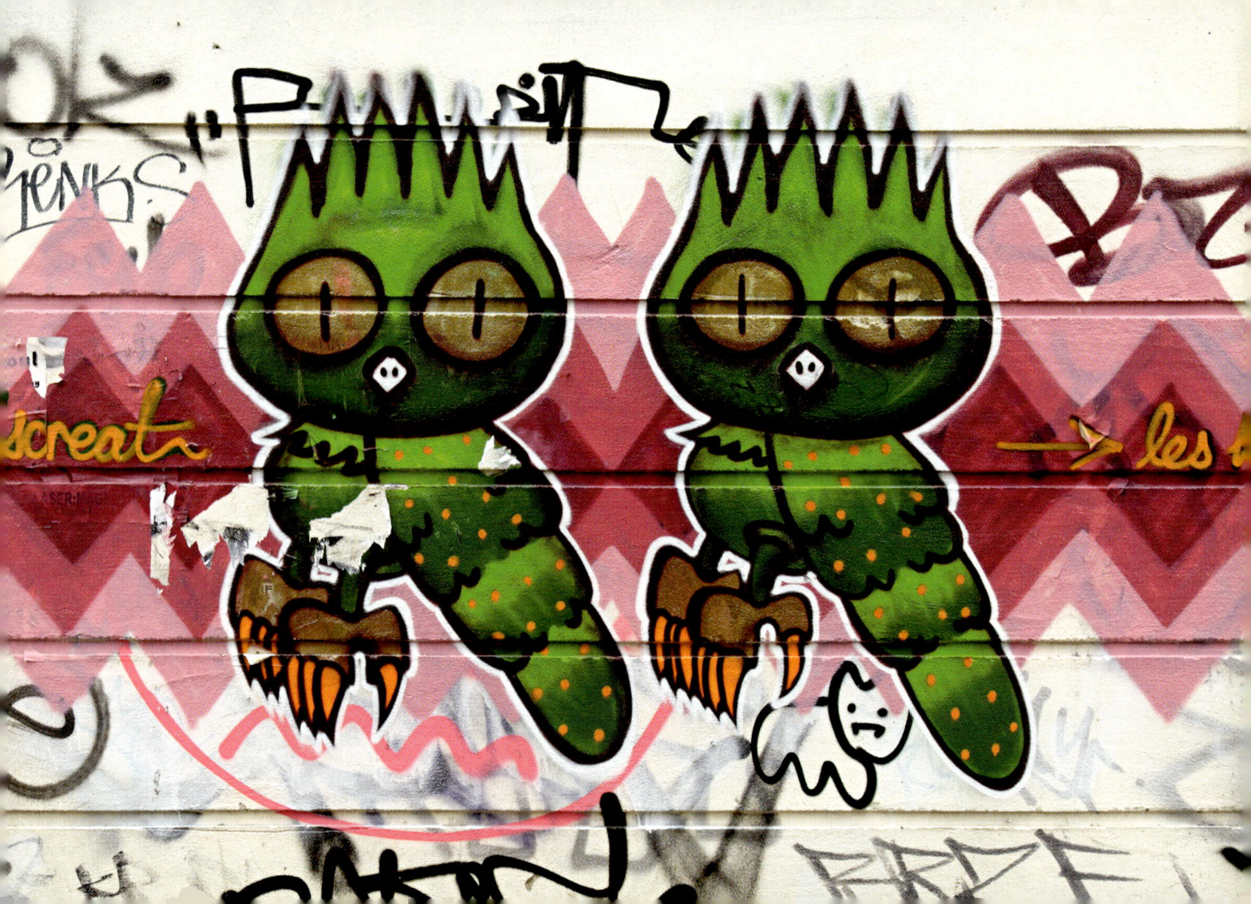
screat
→ les

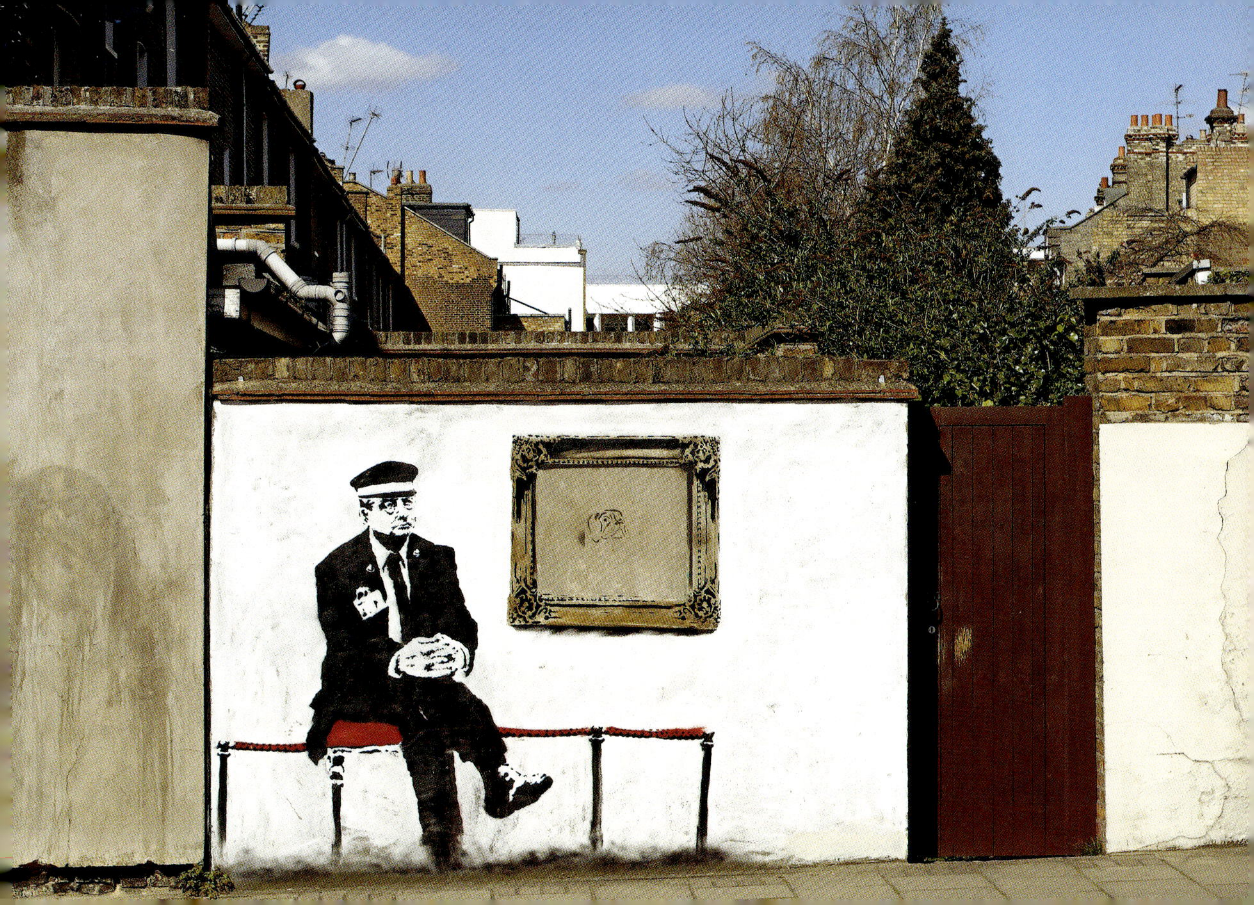

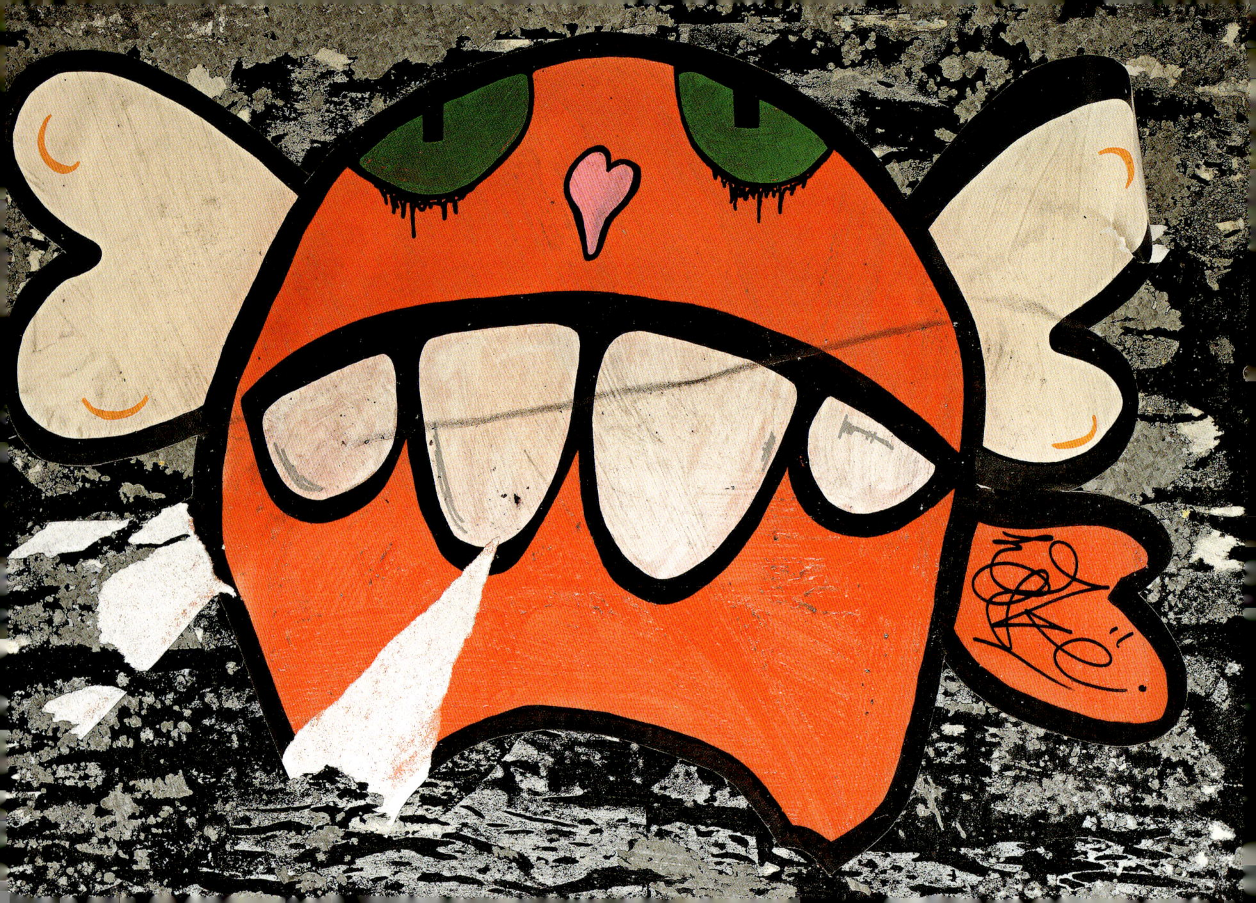

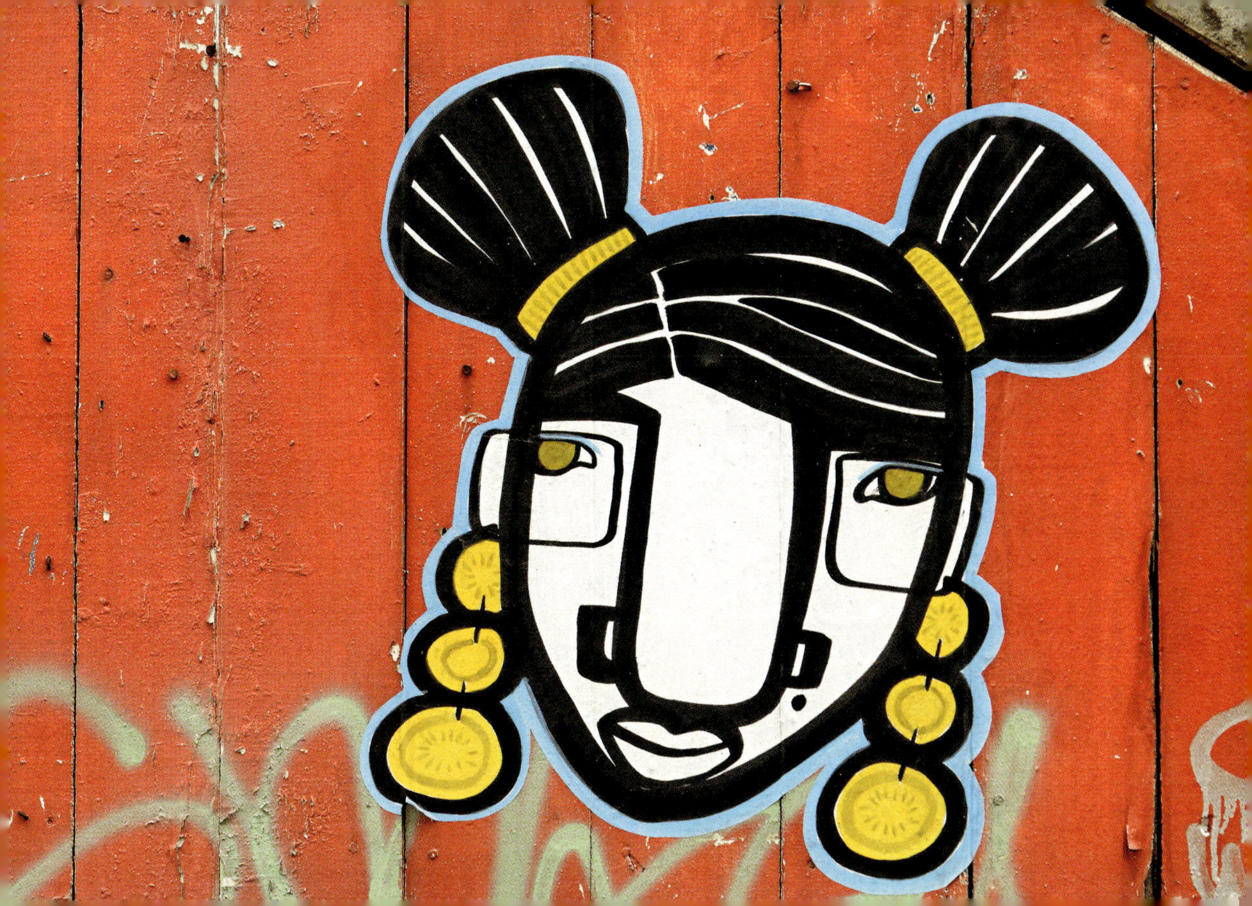

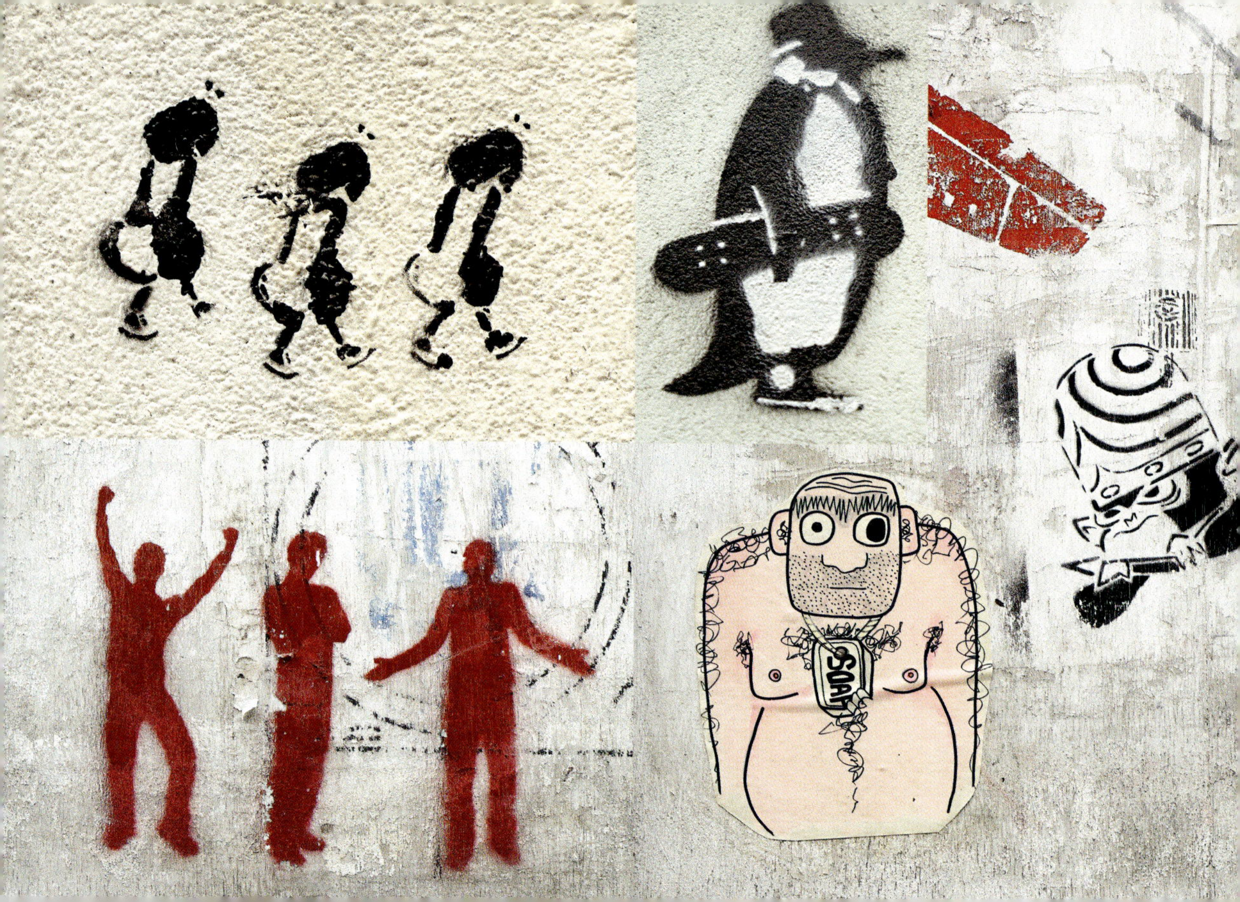
SOAP

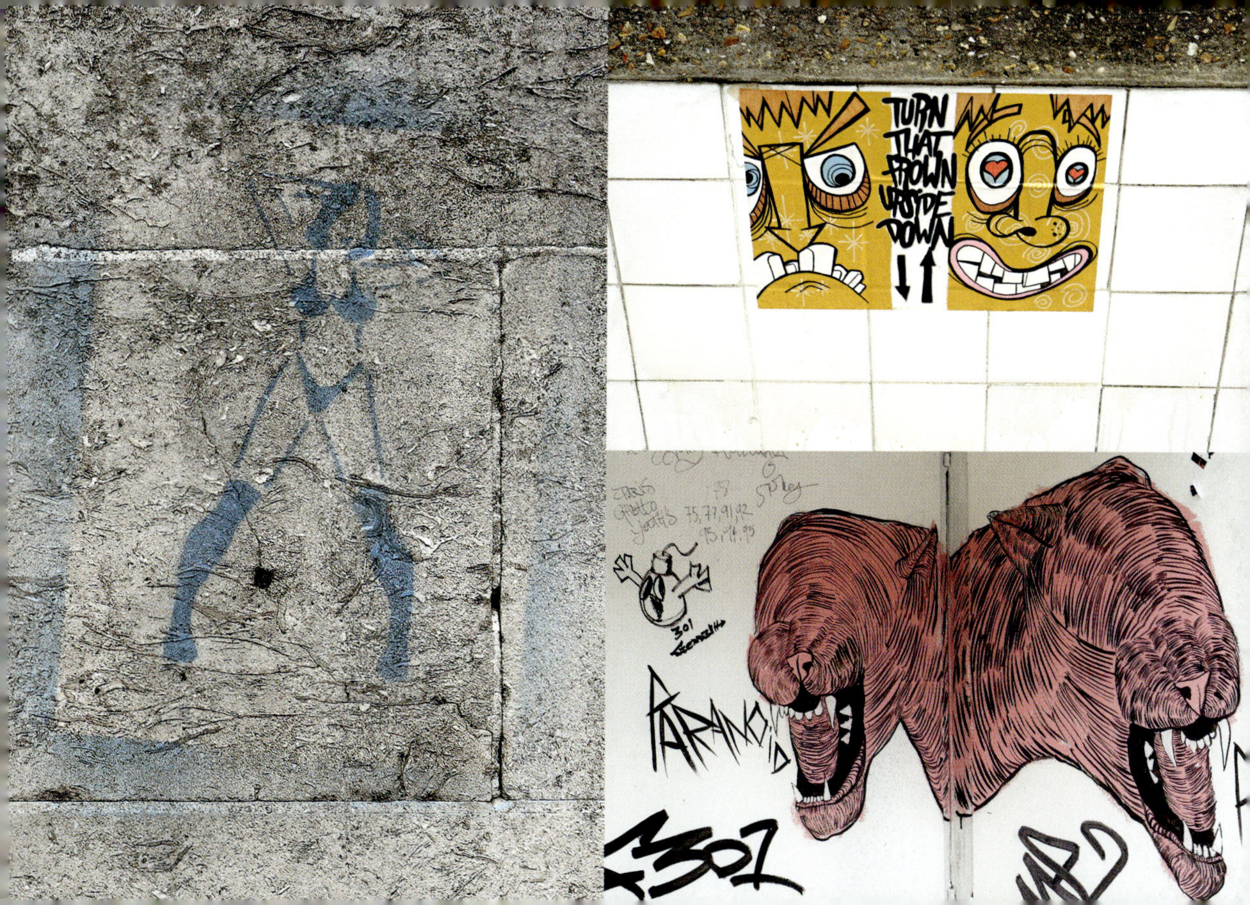
TURN
THAT
FROWN
UPSIDE
DOWN
PARANOID

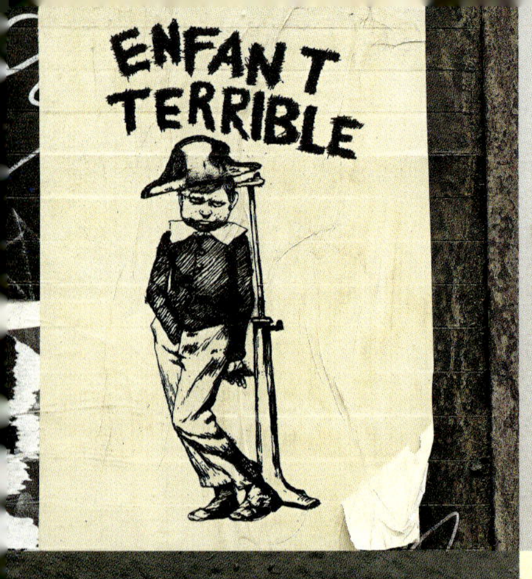
ENFANT TERRIBLE

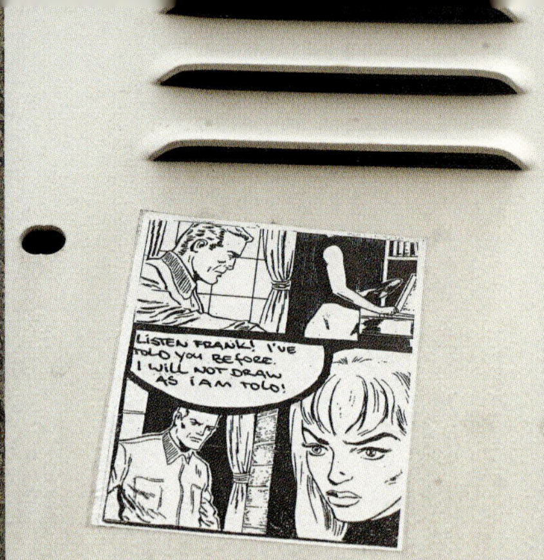
LISTEN FRANK! I'VE TOLD YOU BEFORE. I WILL NOT DRAW AS I AM TOLD!

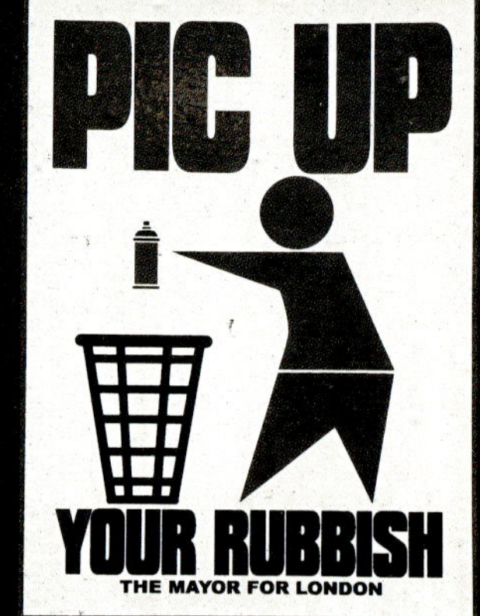
PIC UP
YOUR RUBBISH
THE MAYOR FOR LONDON

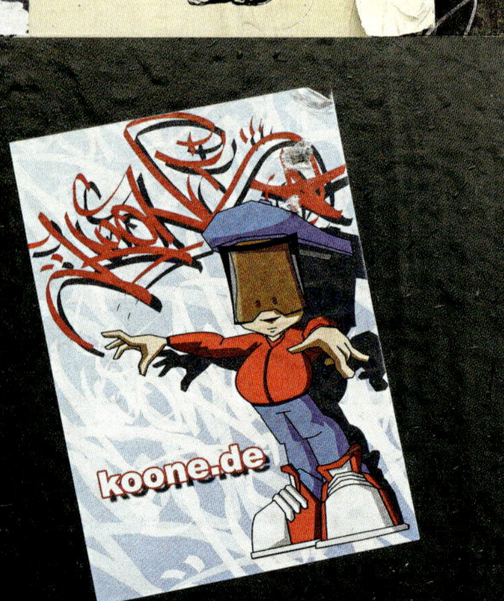
koone.de

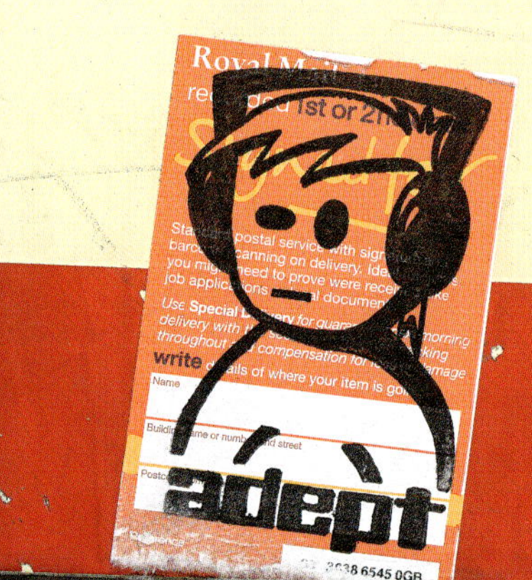
adept

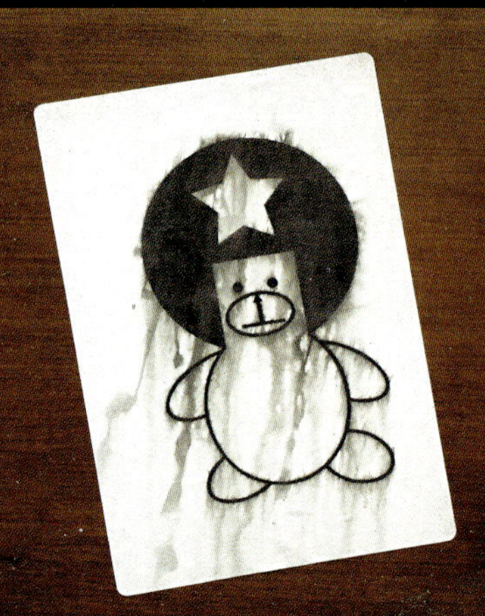

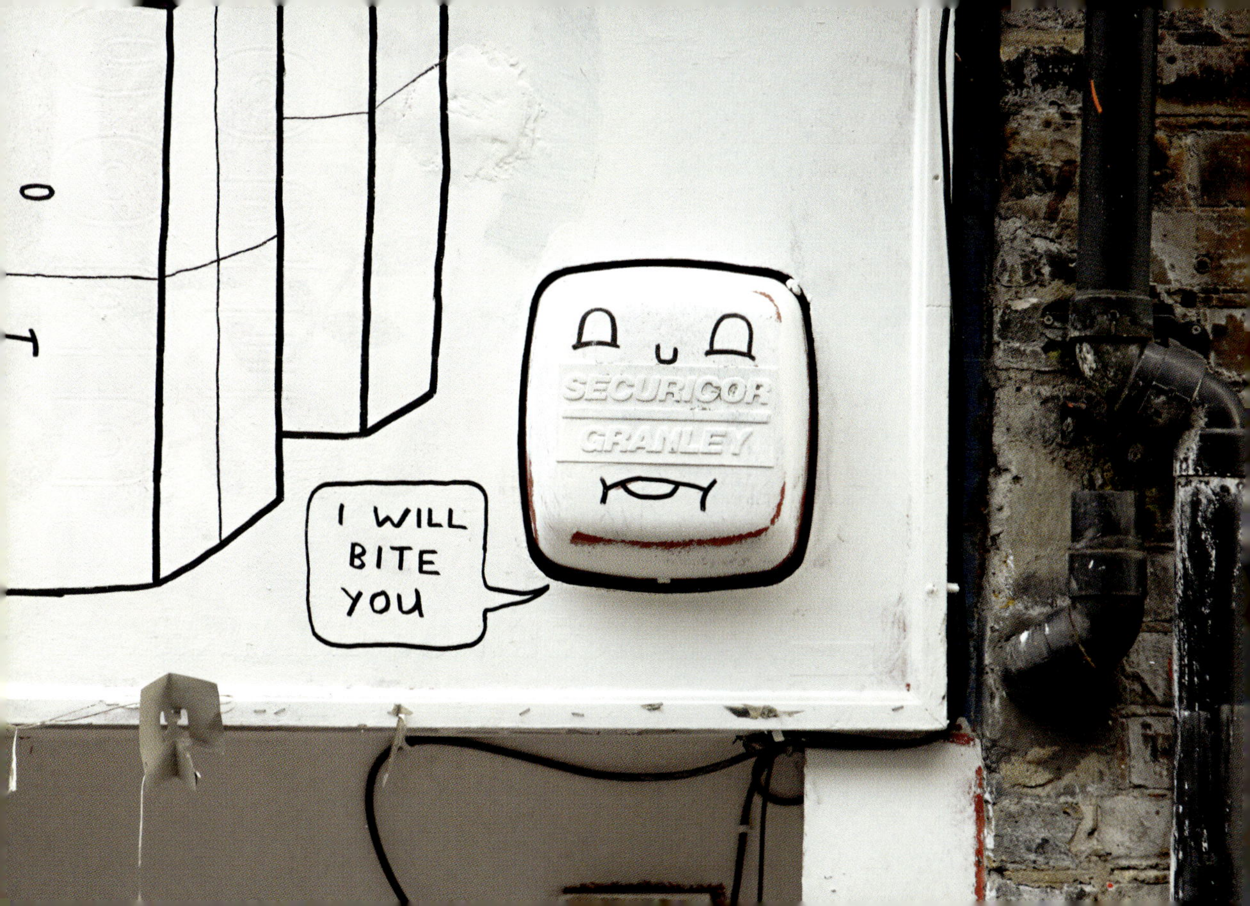
SECURICOR
GRANLEY
I WILL BITE YOU

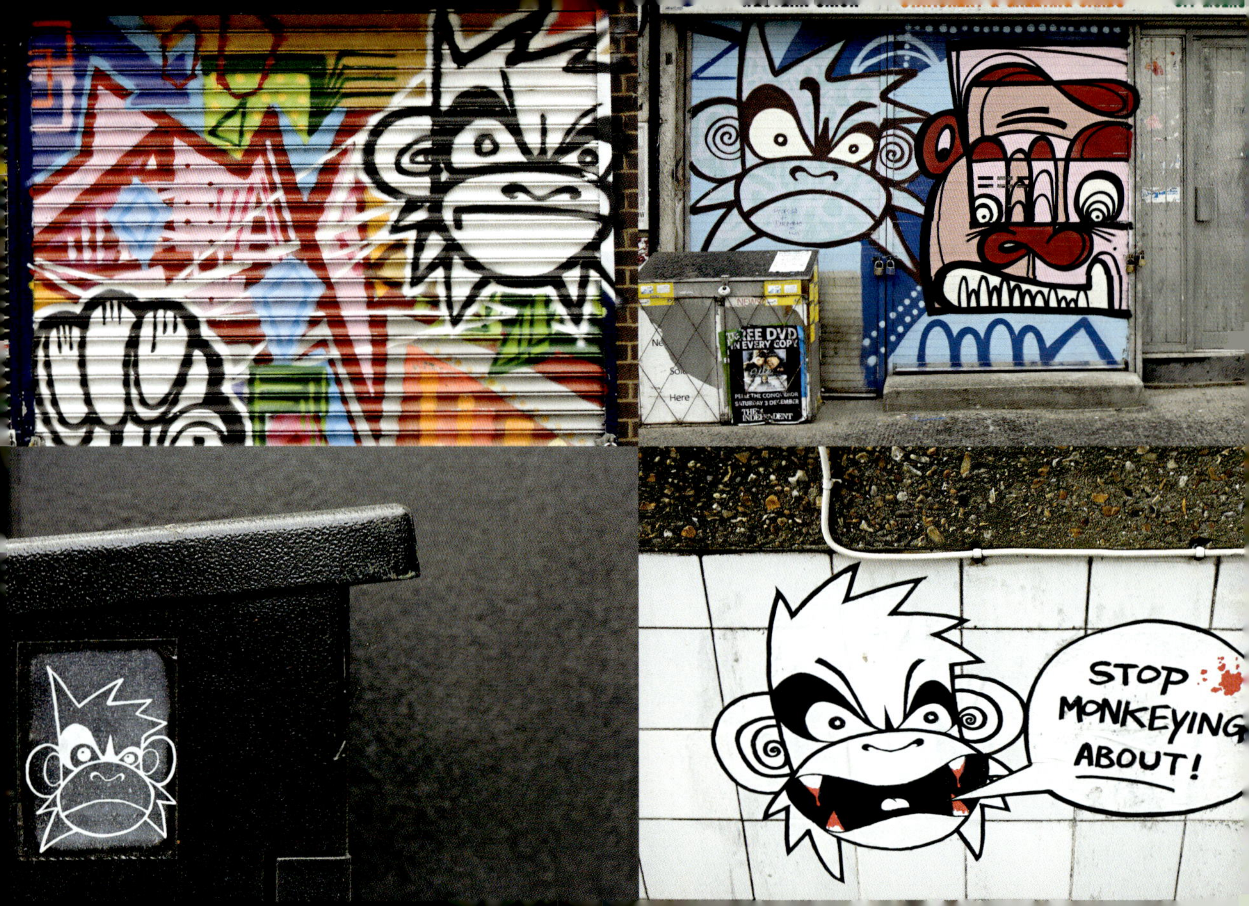
IN EVERY COPY
SATURDAY 3 DECEMBER
Here
STOP MONKEYING ABOUT!

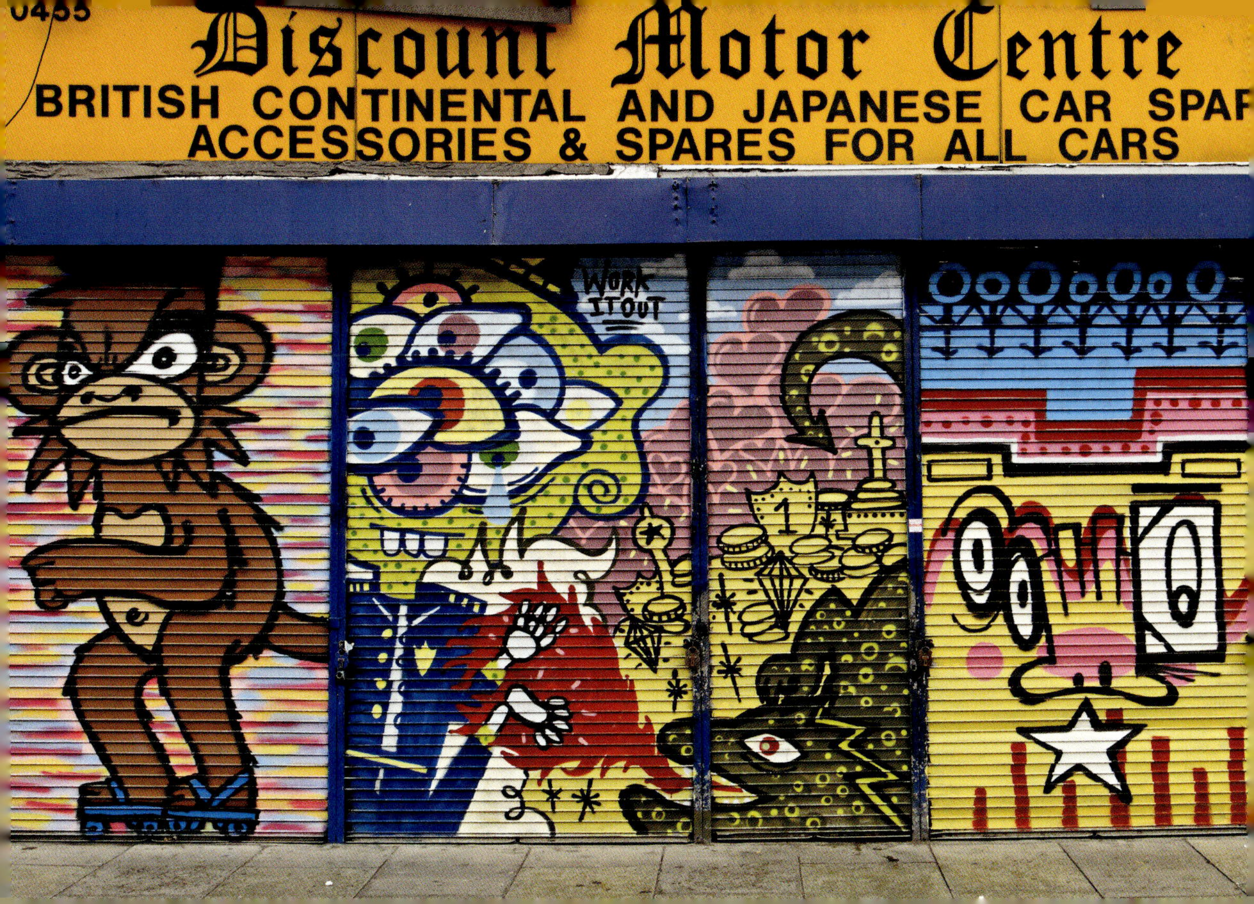

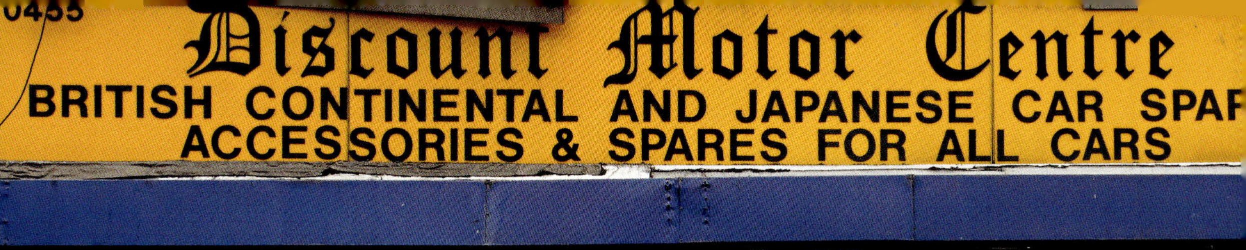
Discount Motor Centre
BRITISH CONTINENTAL AND JAPANESE CAR SPAR
ACCESSORIES & SPARES FOR ALL CARS
WORK IT OUT

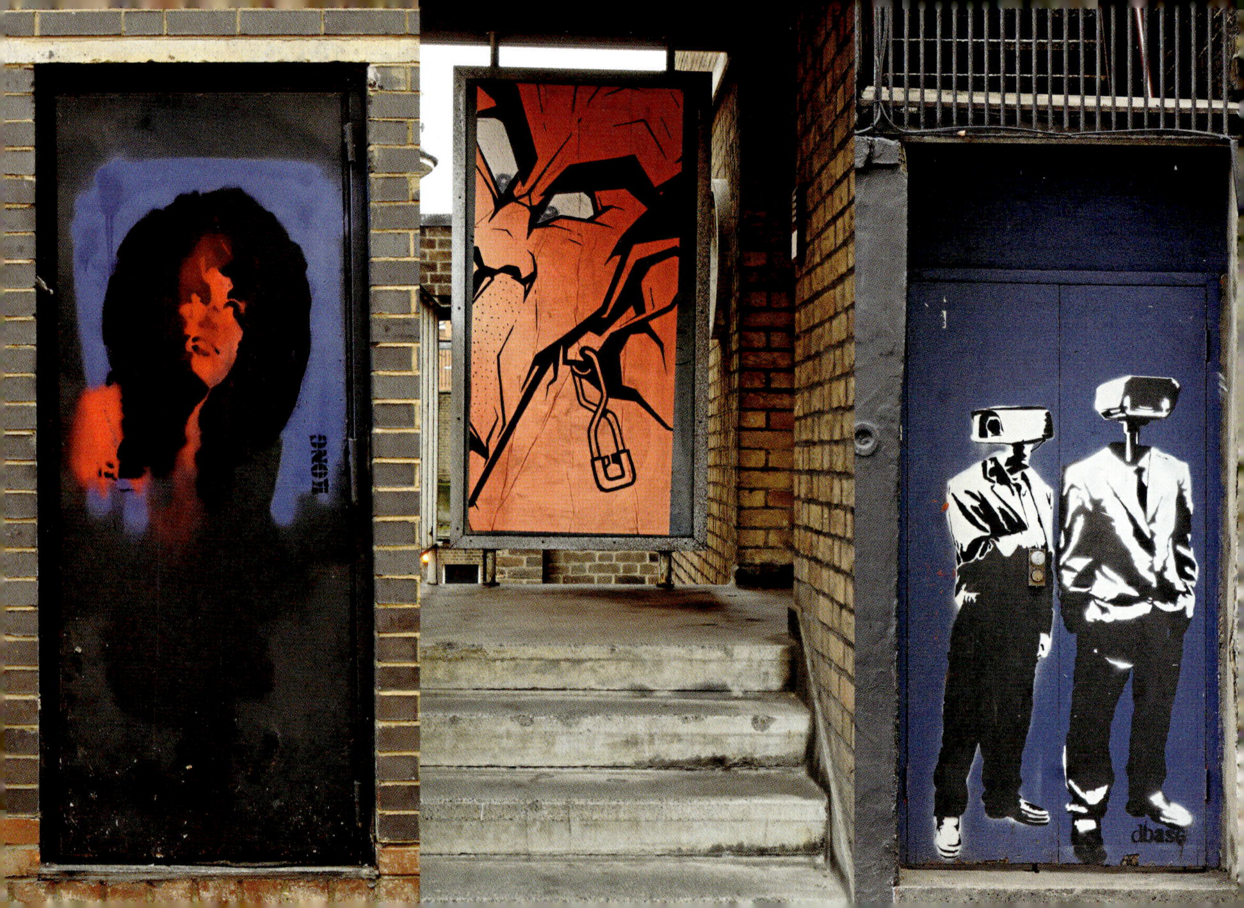
KONG
dbase

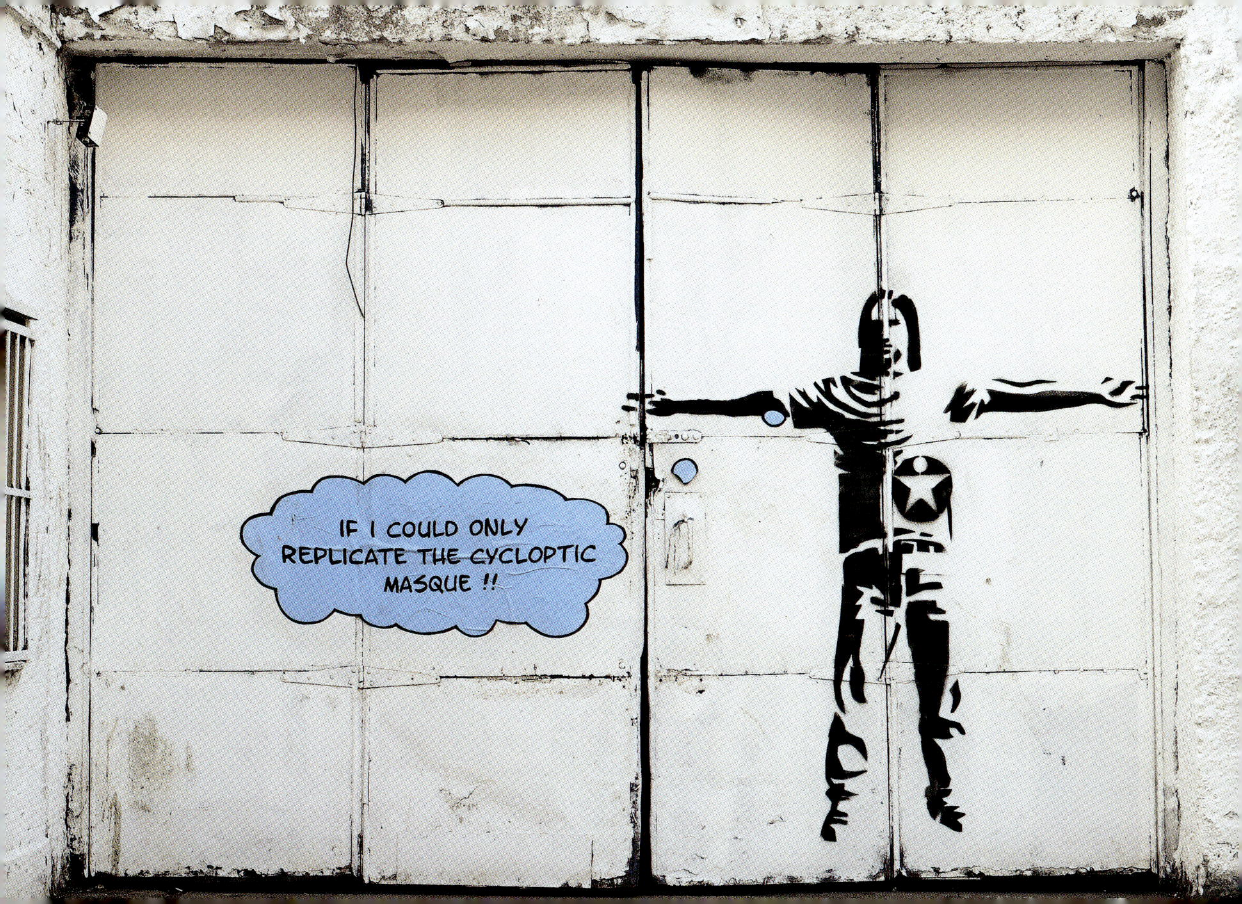
IF I COULD ONLY REPLICATE THE CYCLOPTIC MASQUE !!

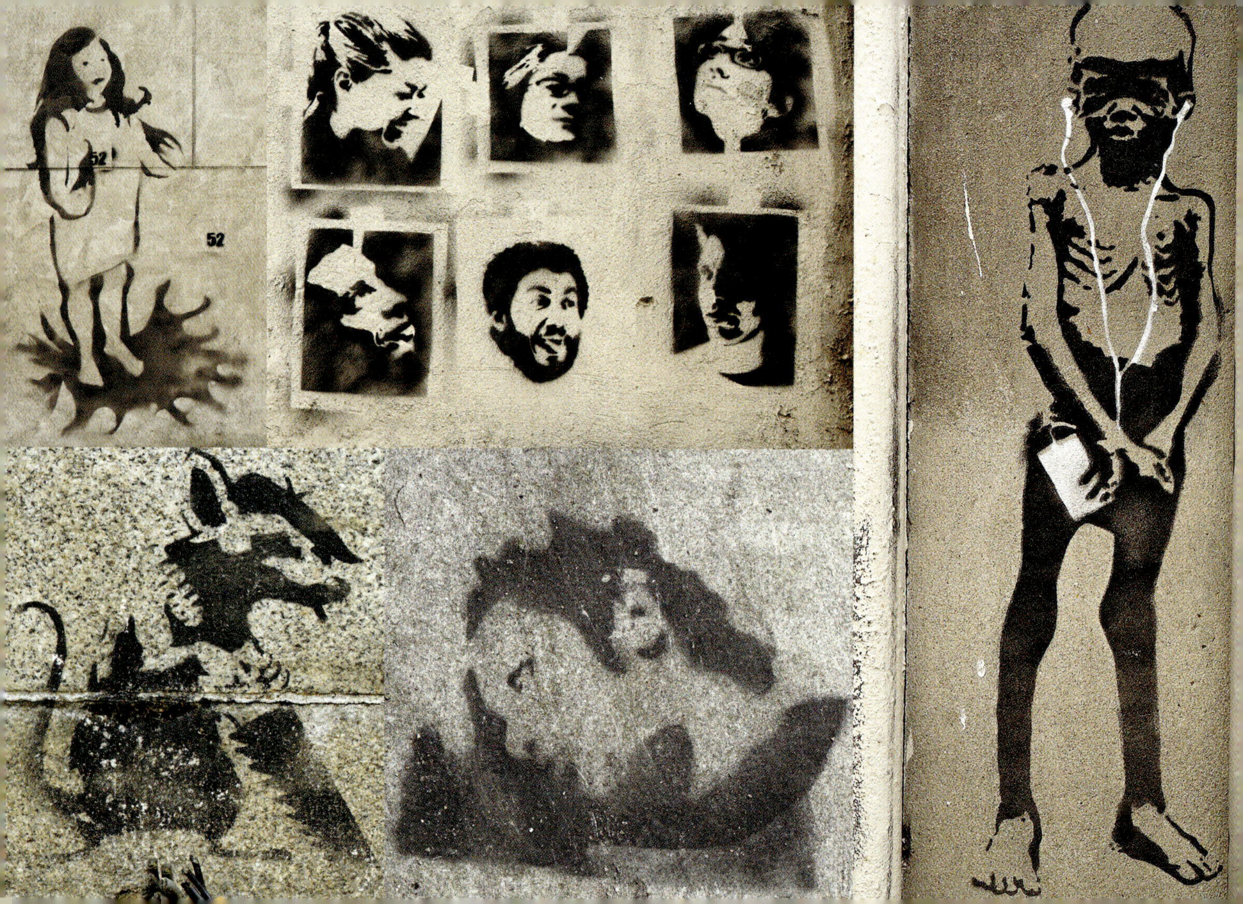
52
52

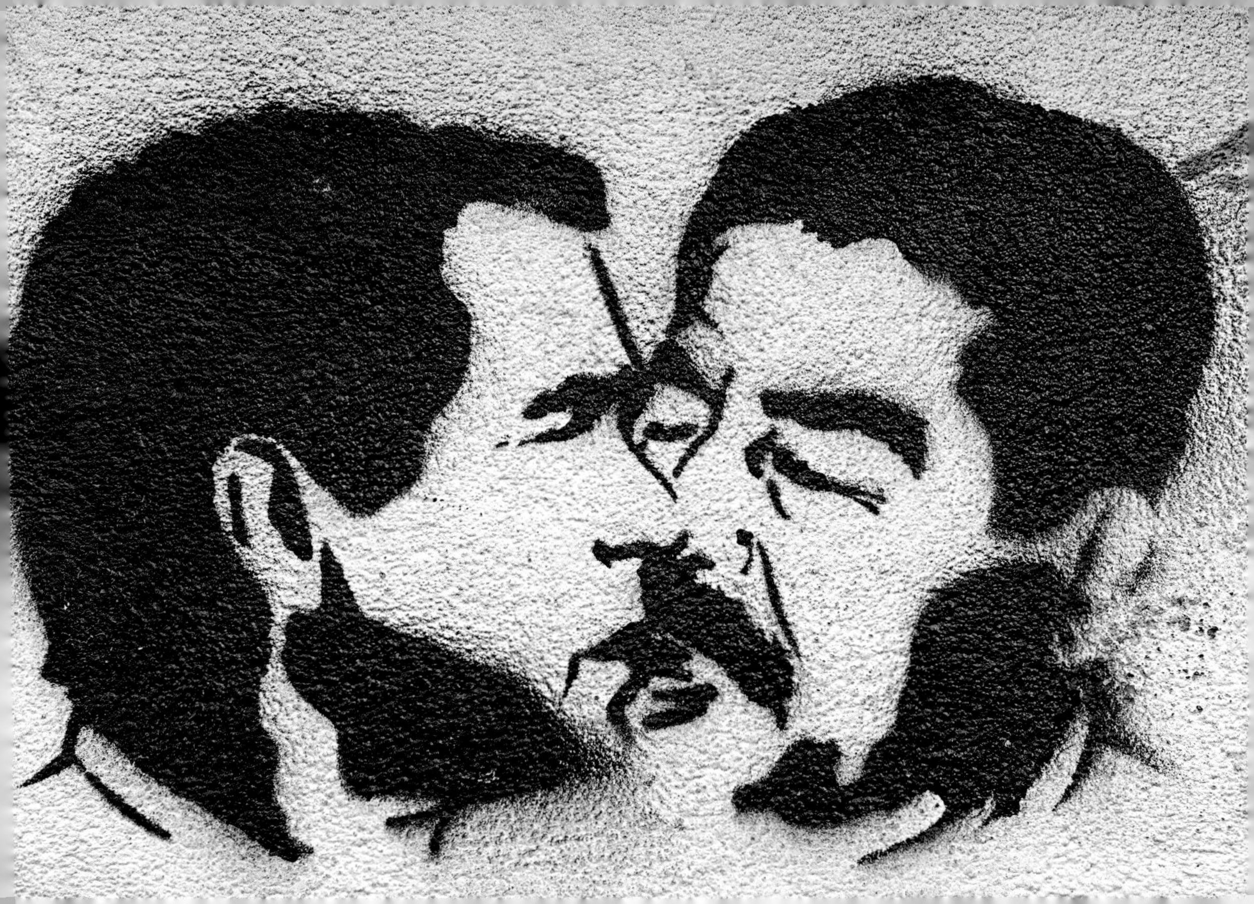

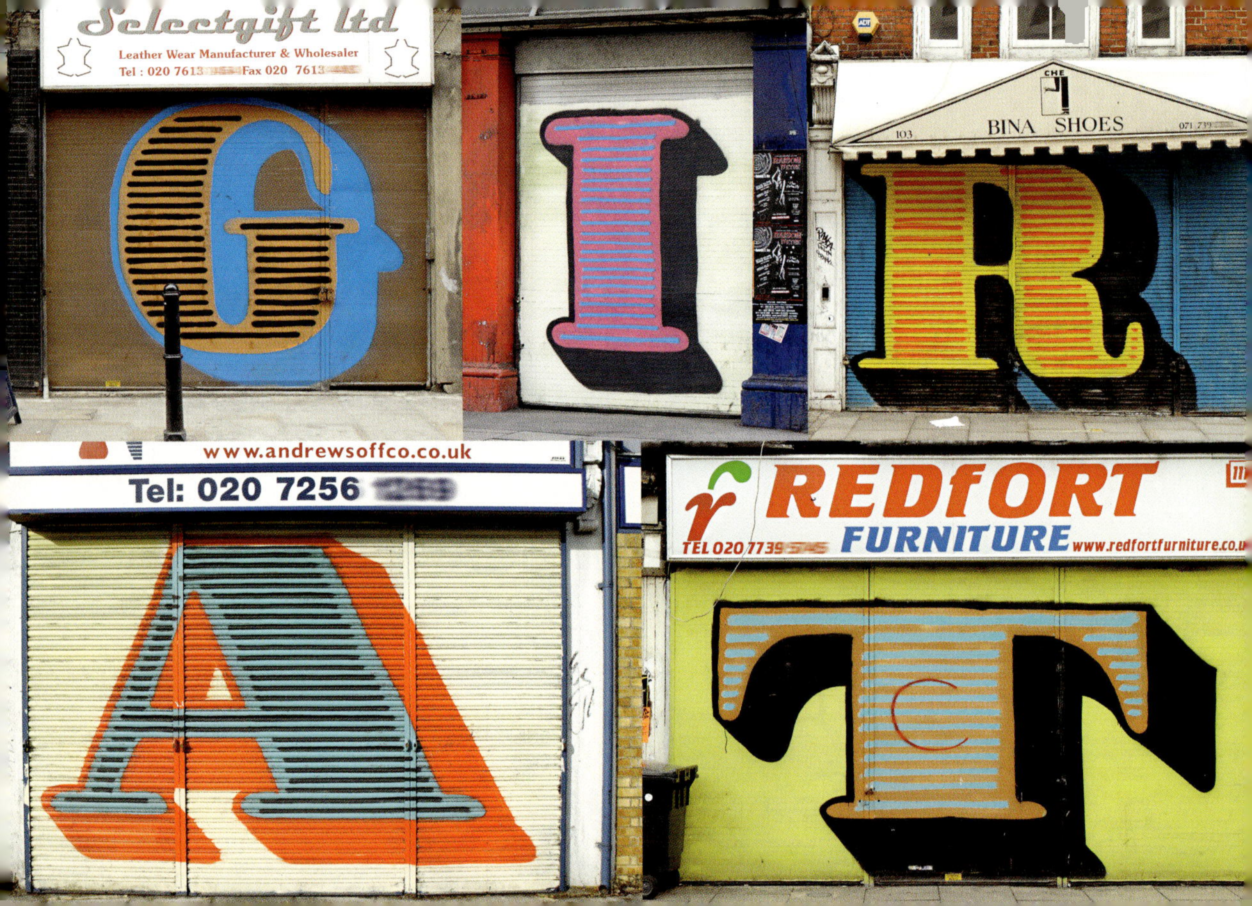

Selectgift ltd
Leather Wear Manufacturer & Wholesaler
Tel : 020 7613 Fax 020 7613
G
I
BINA SHOES
103
R
www.andrewsoffco.co.uk
Tel: 020 7256
A
REDfORT
FURNITURE
TEL 020 7739
www.redfortfurniture.co.u
T

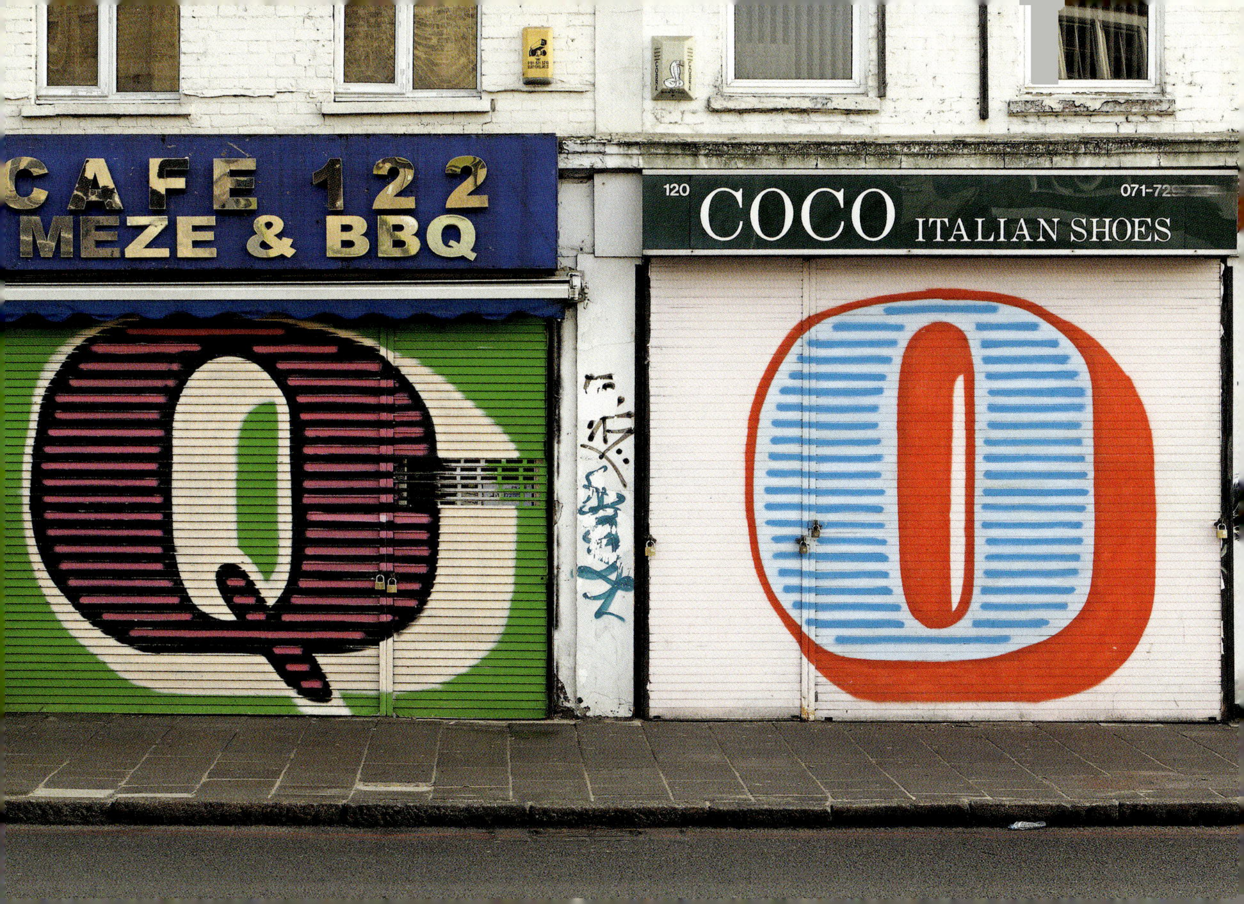
CAFE 122
MEZE & BBQ
120
COCO
ITALIAN SHOES

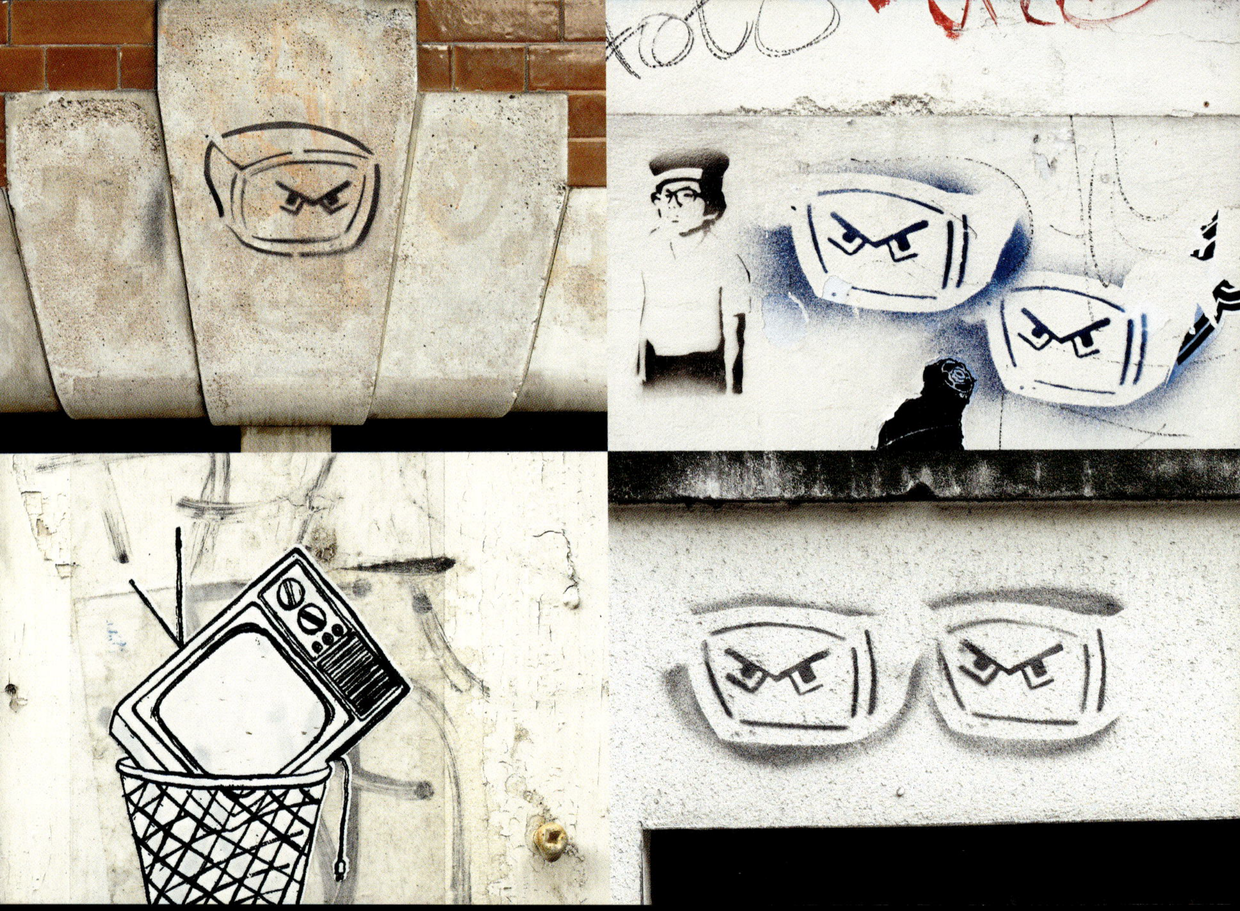

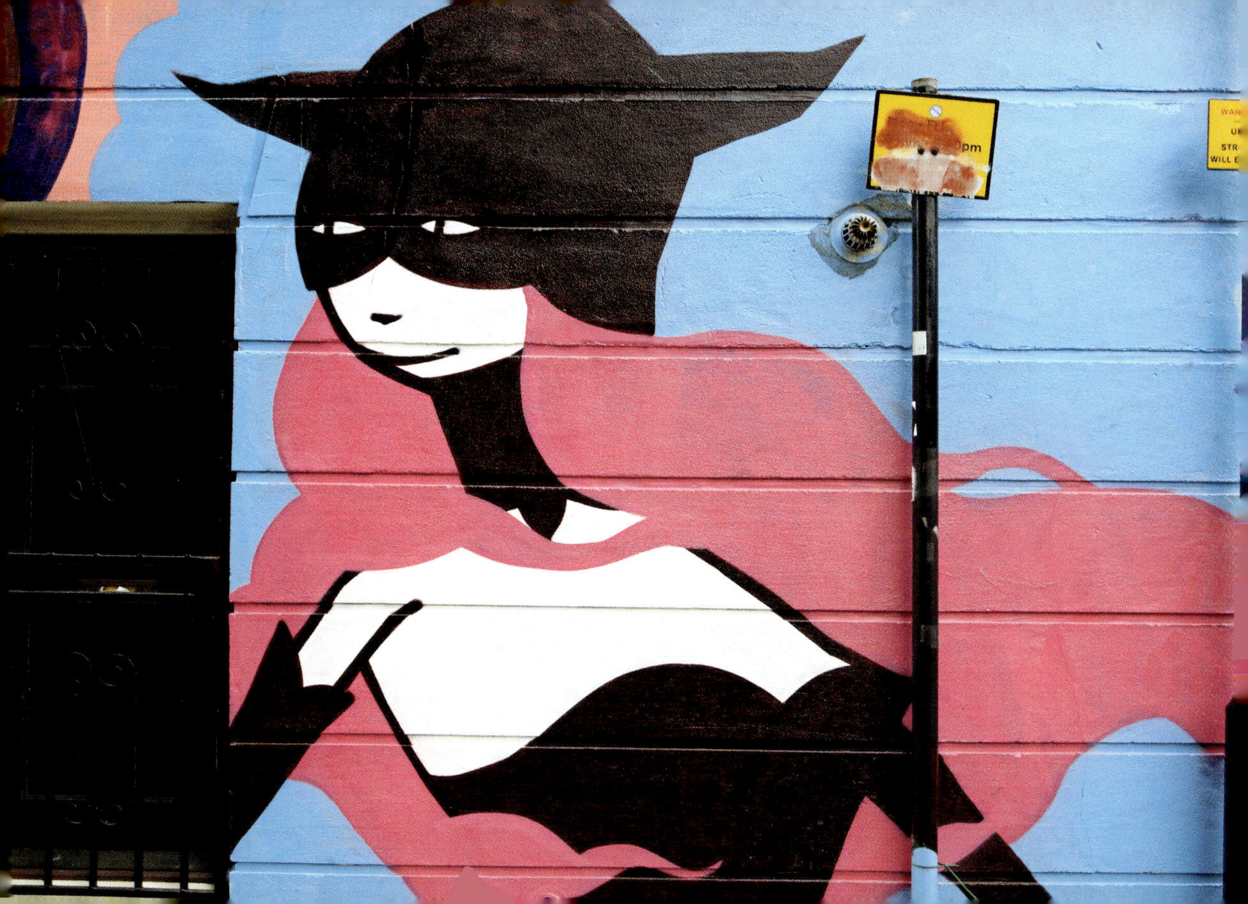

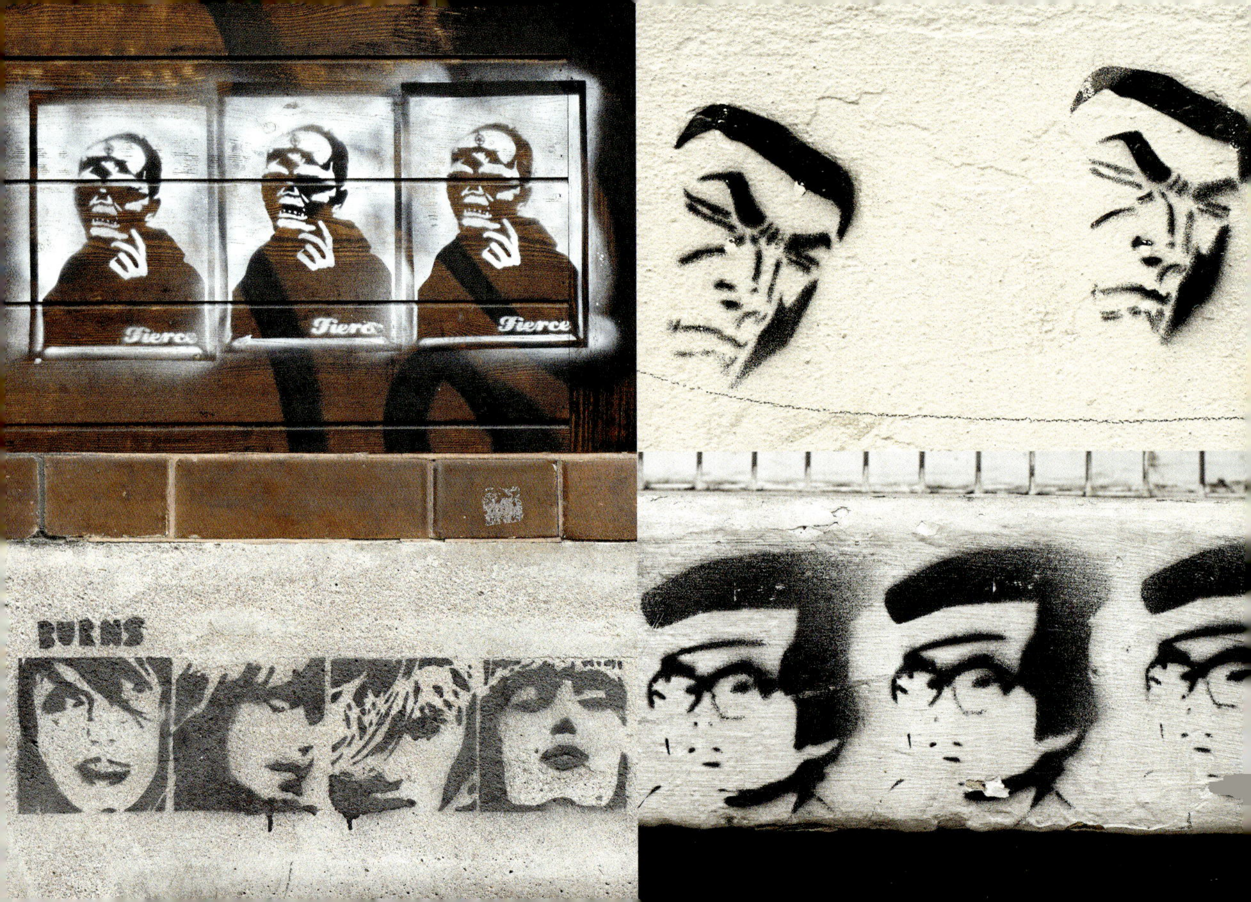

Fierce
Fierce
Fierce
BURNS

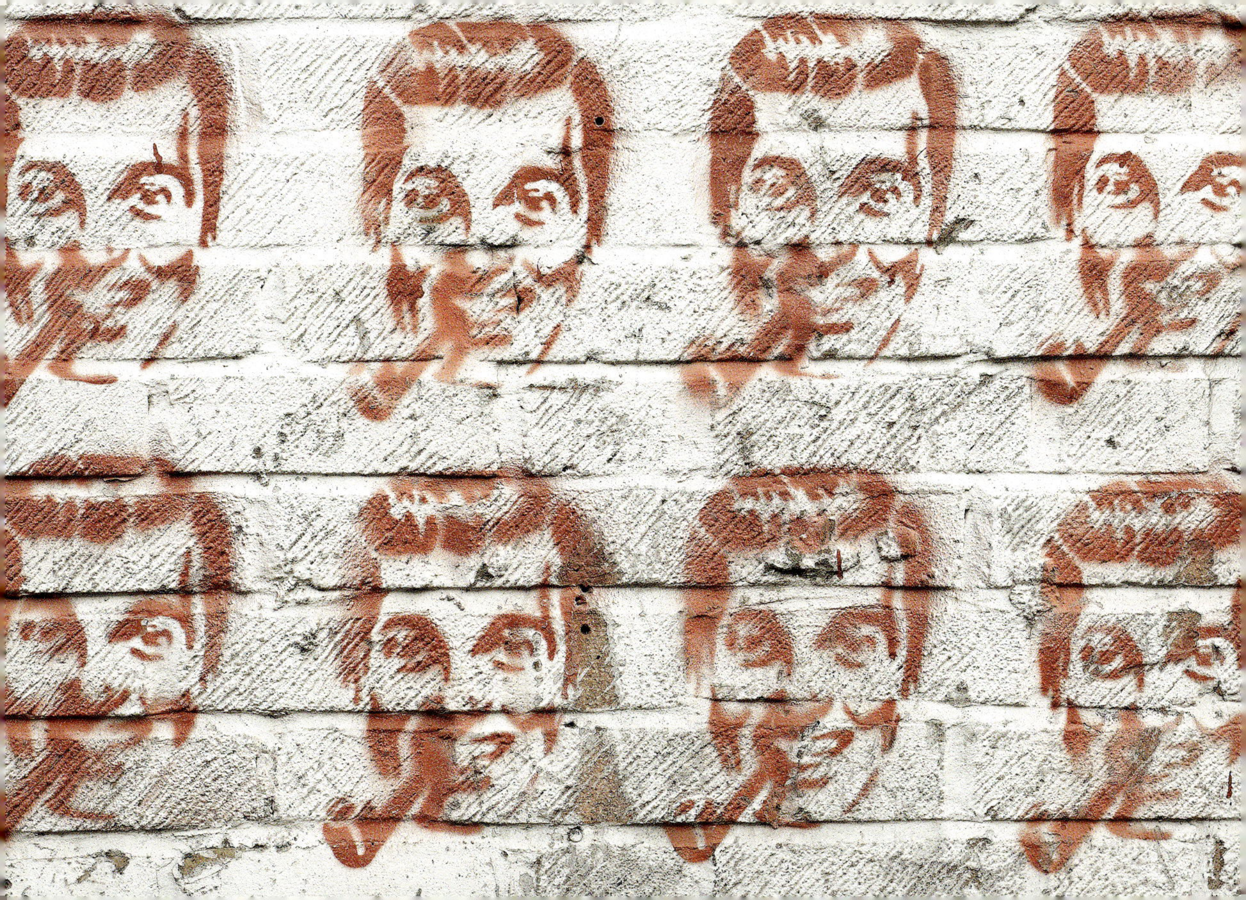

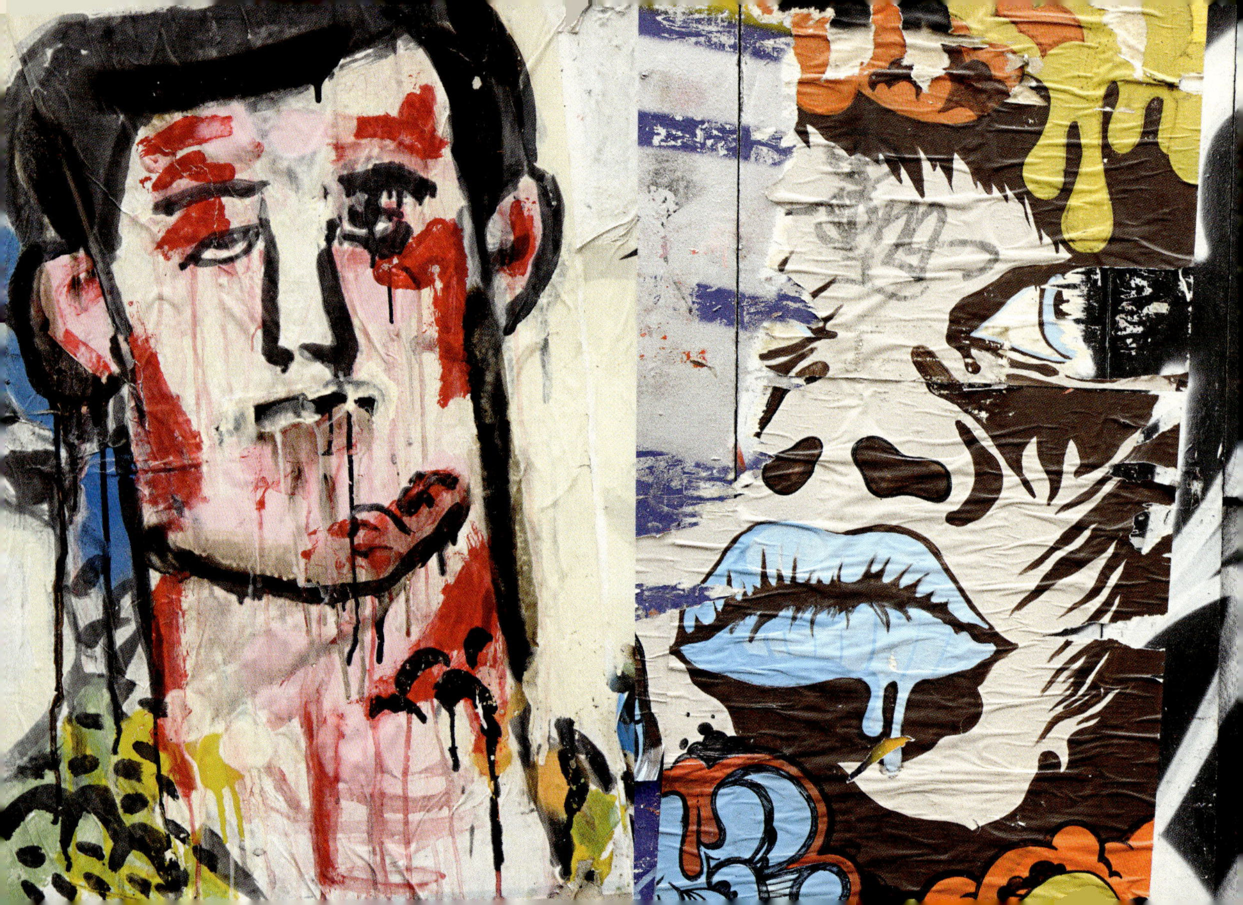

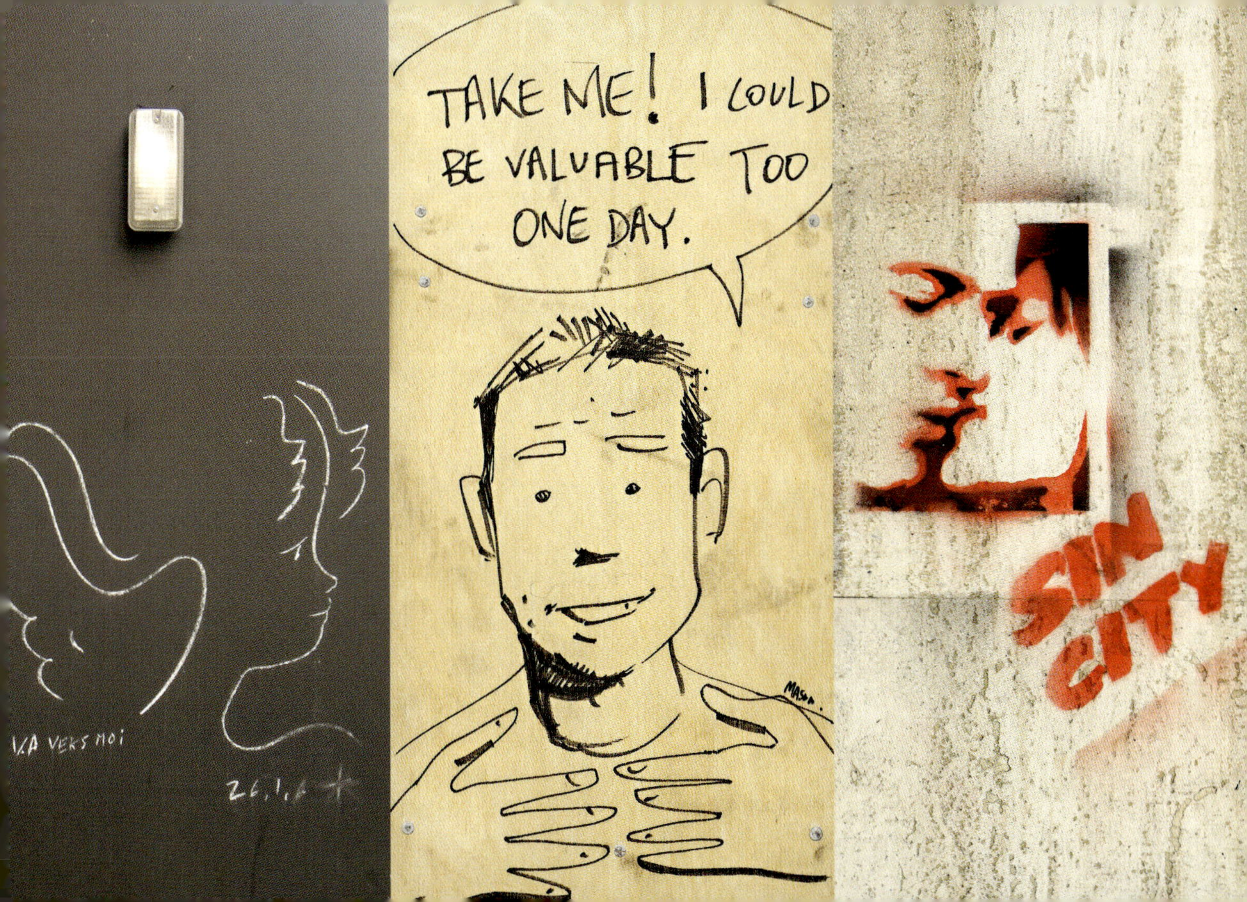
VA VERS MOI
TAKE ME! I COULD BE VALUABLE TOO ONE DAY.
SIN CITY

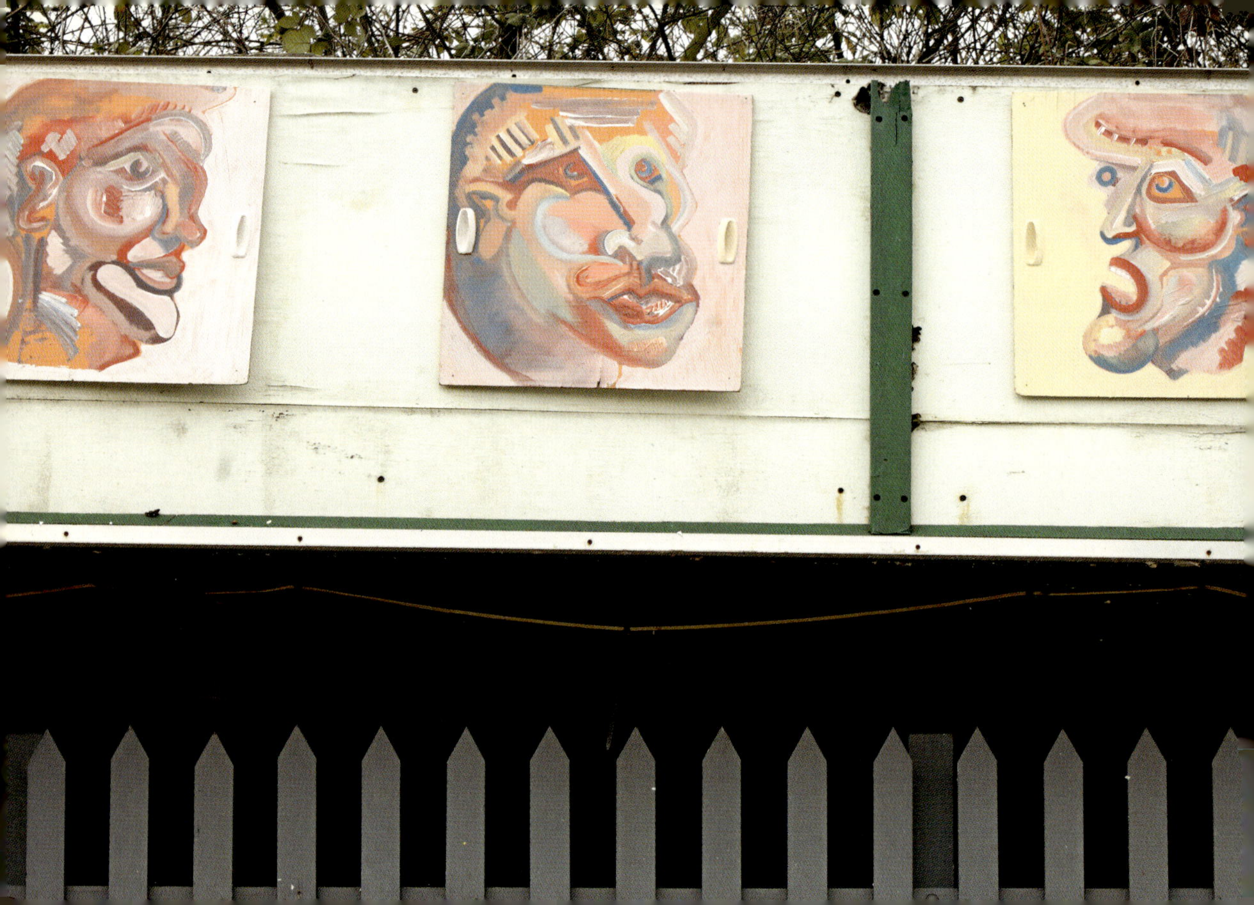

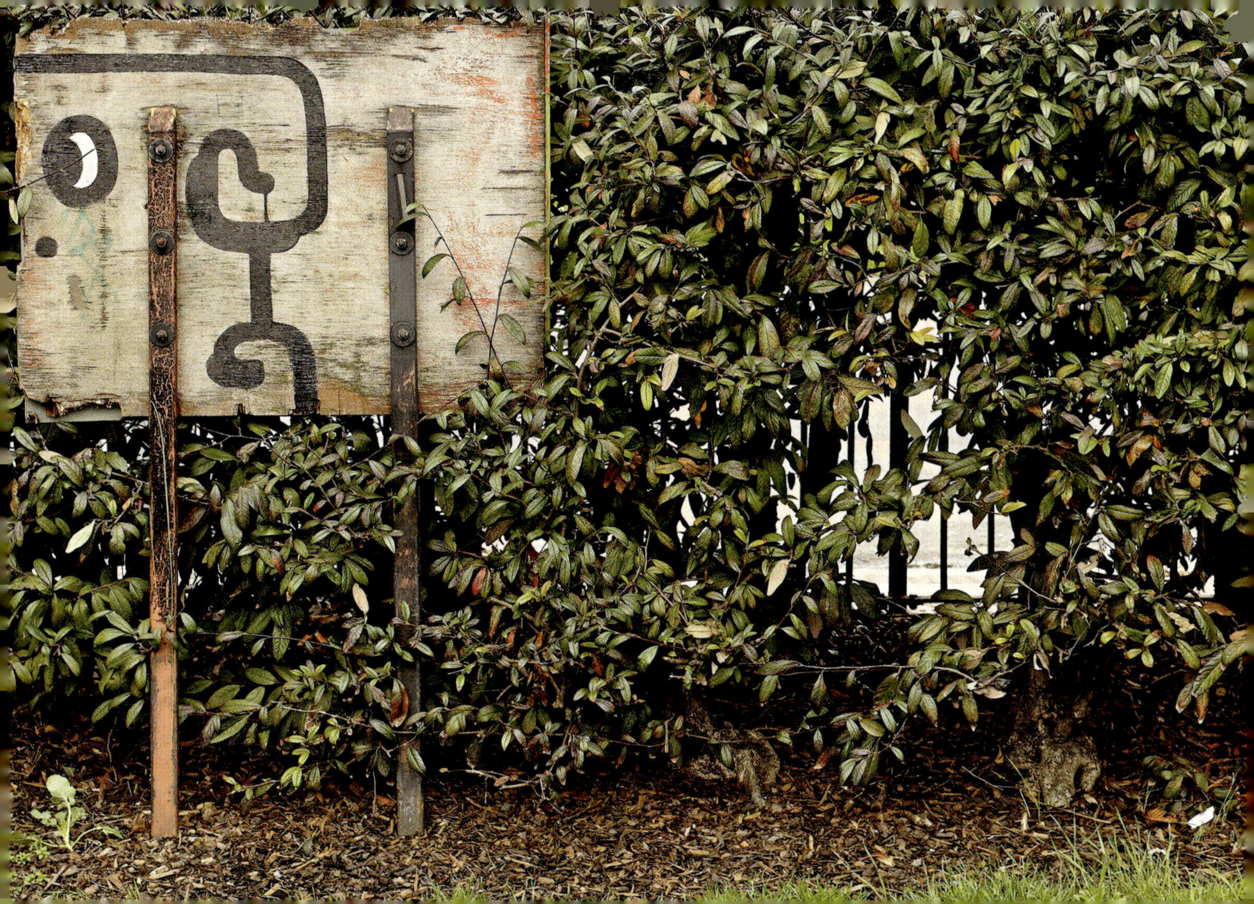

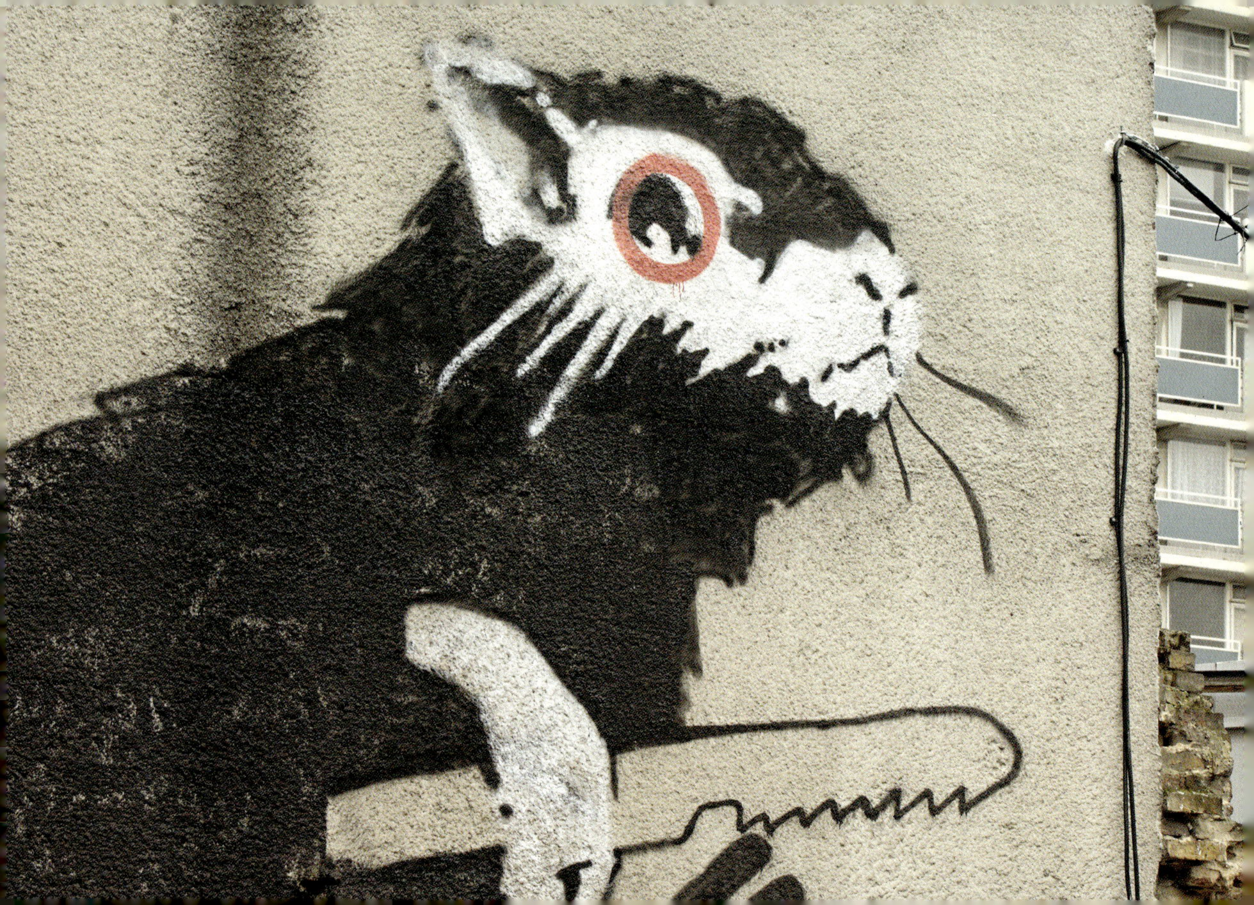

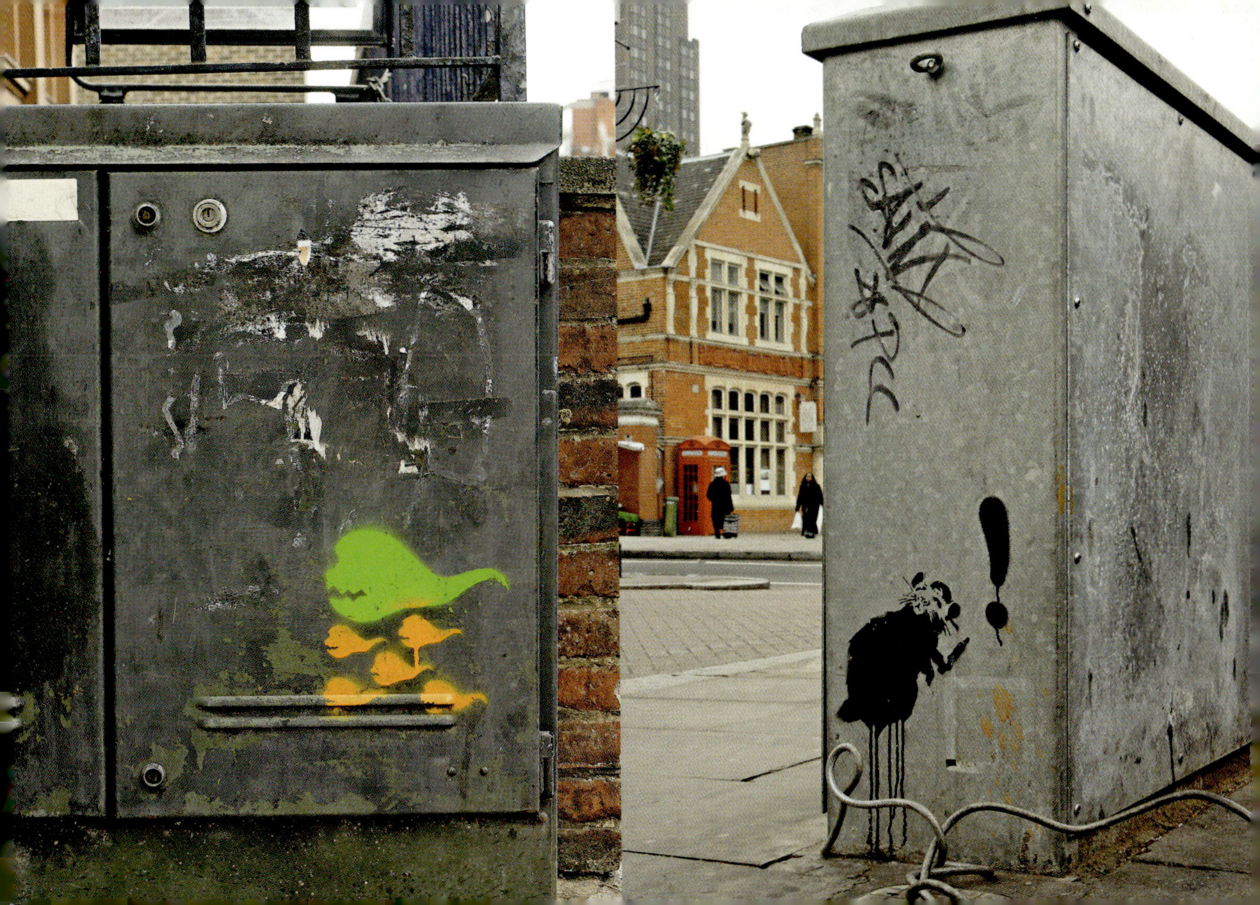

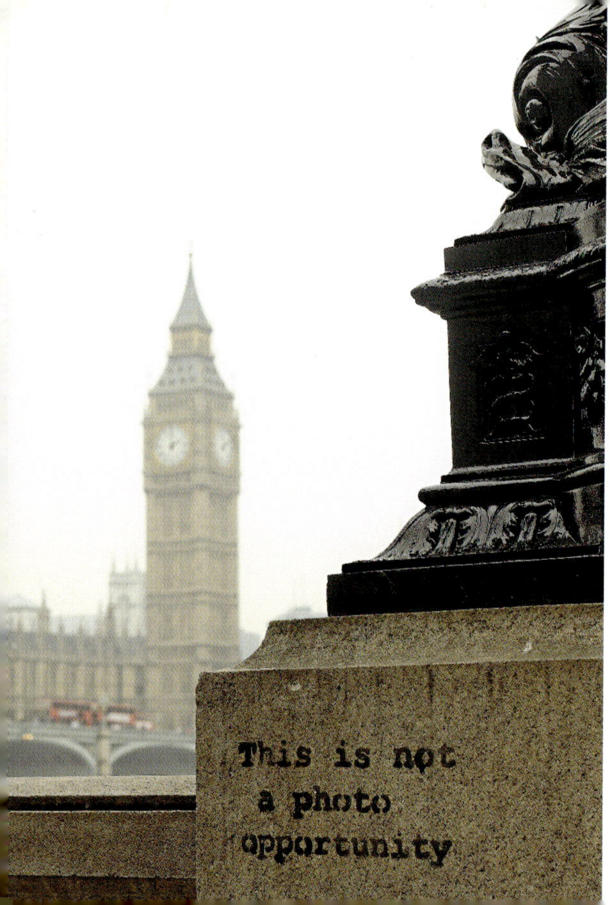

To the three most important women in my life:
my mum, my sister and Sara.

Library of Congress Control Number is available. British Library Cataloguing-in-Publication Data: A catalogue record for this book is available from the British Library. The Deutsche Bibliothek holds a record of this publication in the Deutsche Nationalbibliographie; detailed bibliographical data can be found under: http://dnb.dde.de

Prestel, a member of Verlagsgruppe Random House GmbH
Prestel Verlag
Königinstrasse 9
D-80539 Munich
Tel. +49 (89) 24 29 08-300
Fax +49 (89) 24 29 08-335
www.prestel.de

Prestel Publishing Ltd.
4 Bloomsbury Place
London WC1A 2QA
Tel. +44 (020) 7323-5004
Fax +44 (020) 7636-8004

Prestel Publishing
900 Broadway, Suite 603
New York, N.Y. 10003
Tel. +1 (212) 995-2720
Fax +1 (212) 995-2733
www.prestel.com

Prestel books are available worldwide. Please contact your nearest bookseller or one of the above addresses for information concerning your local distributor.

Editorial direction: Philippa Hurd
Design and layout: René Güttler
Origination: Reproline Mediateam,
Printing: Tlačiarne BB, spol. sr.o.

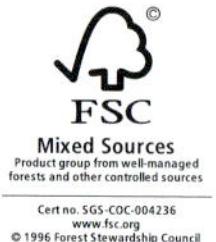

Verlagsgruppe Random House FSC-DEU-0100
The FSC-certified paper Novatech has been supplied by Antalis.

ISBN 978-3-7913-3674-9

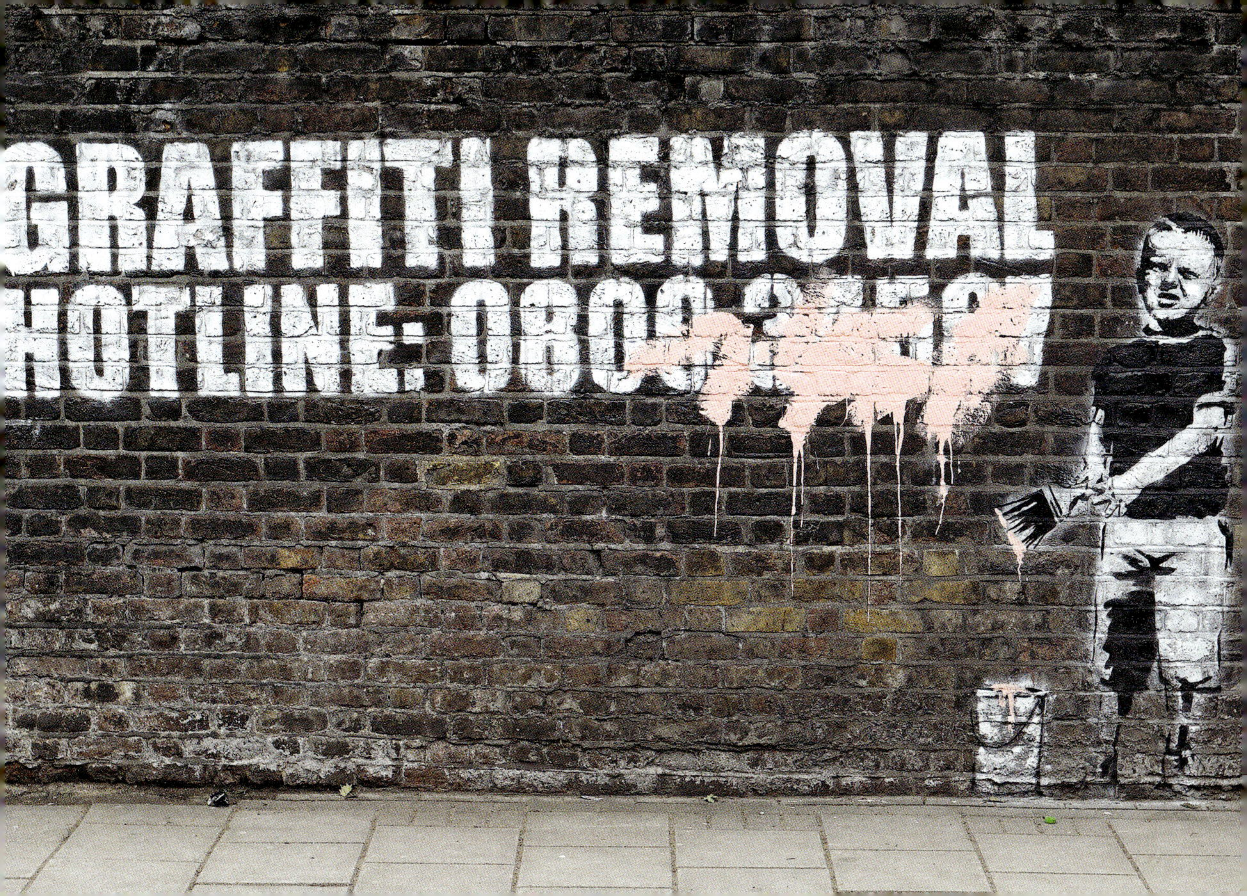
GRAFFITI REMOVAL
HOTLINE: 080

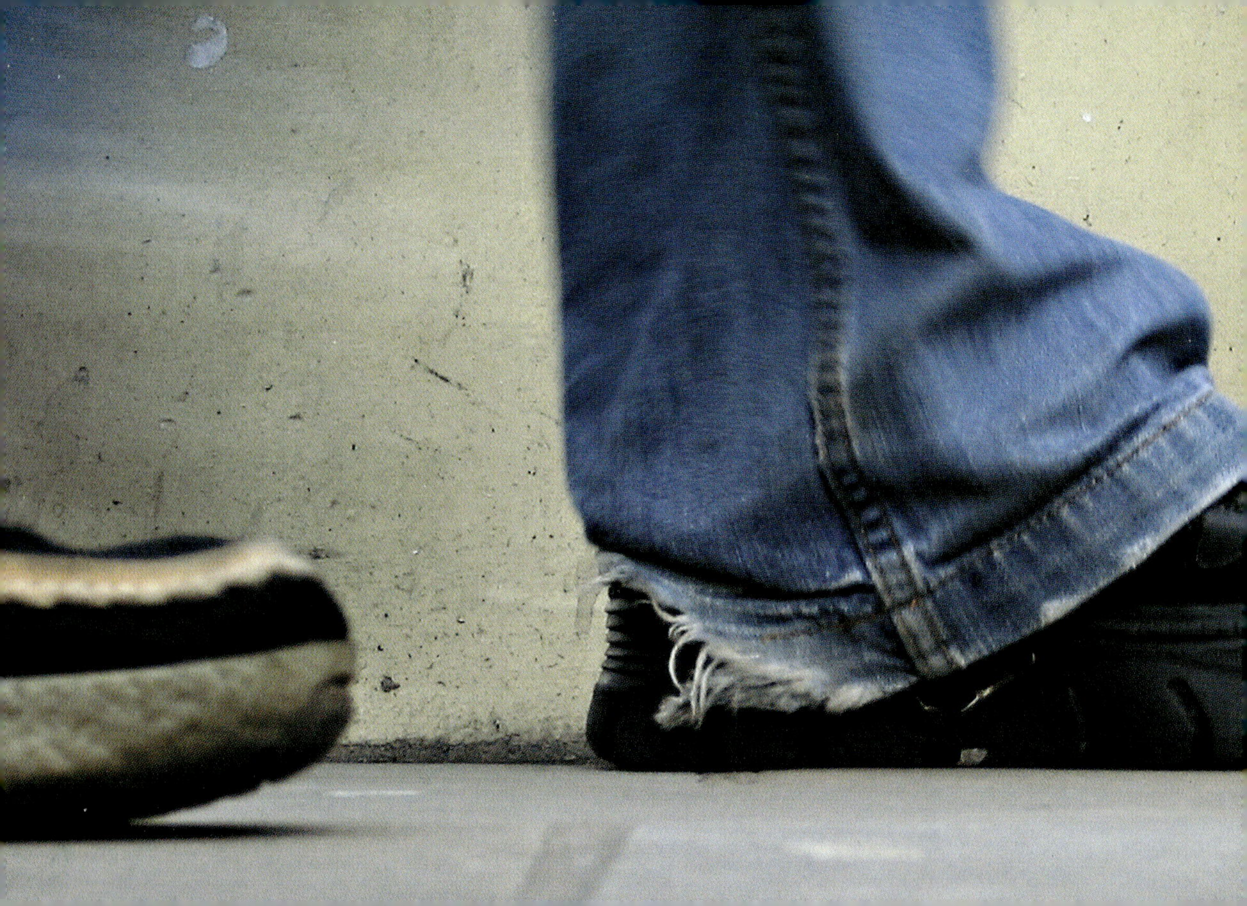